TAXES ARE A WOMAN'S ISSUE

TAXES ARE A WOMAN'S ISSUE
REFRAMING THE DEBATE

MIMI ABRAMOVITZ AND SANDRA MORGEN
WITH THE NATIONAL COUNCIL FOR RESEARCH ON WOMEN

The Feminist Press at the City University of New York

Published by the Feminist Press at the City University of New York
The Graduate Center
365 Fifth Avenue, Suite 5406
New York, NY 10016
www.feministpress.org

Library of Congress Cataloging-in-Publication Data

Abramovitz, Mimi.
    Taxes are a woman's issue : reframing the debate / Mimi Abramovitz
  and Sandra Morgen with the National Council for Research on Women.
      p. cm.
    ISBN-13: 978-1-55861-522-9 (pbk.)
    ISBN-10: 1-55861-522-9 (pbk.)
    1. Women—Taxation—United States.   2. Taxation—United States.
  I. Morgen, Sandra.   II. National Council for Research on Women (U.S.)
  III. Title.
  HJ2362.A27 2006
  336.20082'0973—dc22

                                                                    2005032358

This publication was made possible, in part, by private donations by Mariam K. Chamberlain, Sheila Hafter Gray, and Mary E. Rubin and Samuel A. Lieber.

Text and cover design by Lisa Force
Printed in Canada by Transcontinental

11 10 09 08 07 06   5 4 3 2 1

The National Council for Research on Women, along with the Feminist Press and the authors of this book, are deeply honored to dedicate this work to Mariam Chamberlain. Throughout her career as an economist, a philanthropist, and a leader in the academic women's movement, Mariam has unwaveringly supported efforts to expand economic literacy and create greater economic security for people around the globe. Her pioneering vision as a young program officer at the Ford Foundation, her founding and leadership of the National Council for Research on Women, and her continuing support today have given voice to two generations of women scholars and experts and helped transform the lives of women and girls.

CONTENTS

PREFACE

The National Council for Research on Women is releasing this volume at a critical moment for women, for their families, and indeed, for all of us. As a nation, we face war abroad, security threats at home, natural disasters, deep concerns about the nation's economic stability, and deep political and ideological divides. All of these concerns raise fundamental questions about the ways we live together as a society, the role of government, and how we together can support and protect our shared civic, social, and economic life.

Taxes are central to these questions, and with this volume we aim to use the unique and shared experiences of women, across all their diversity, to frame issues, develop strategies, advocate for policies, and act to implement tax and spending policies that serve all the nation's people as well as our shared national goals—in times of extraordinary need as well as in more ordinary times.

Seen through women's eyes, analyzed through their diverse experiences, taxes tell a revealing story about some of the fundamental realities of our economy and our society. They raise questions about deeply ingrained inequities based on gender, race, and class. They suggest new ways of thinking about public services and new strategies for addressing some of the most contentious issues facing us as a nation.

Yes, we all need taxes. They sustain the nation's civil, social, and economic life and provide the resources we need to protect our population, implement our vision of community, and invest in our future. Tax policy reflects the philosophy of our government and the priorities we set for ourselves as a nation. To a great extent, taxes determine the quality of our lives—the safety of the water we drink, the quality of the roads we commute on, the security of our homes and communities, and the vibrancy of our communal life. The issue of taxes goes to the fundamental question of the proper role of government.

Yet taxes also reflect the fundamental inequities in our society, the different ways that people of different races, classes, and gender access opportunities and participate in our national life. By bringing a gendered lens to the issue of taxation—by seeing taxes through women's diverse experiences and perspectives—we can see how those structural inequities play out at all levels of our economy. We can analyze them in terms of the ways we raise money for public services and the ways we spend it. This is because women, despite their great diversity, share a certain position in our economy, whatever their social or economic class. And in many cases, they share the inequities and injustices rendered by a tax system that was created without their work, their needs, or their lives in mind.

With this volume, the National Council for Research on Women is calling for a comprehensive discussion of how these inequities operate, and how they affect all of us. How does current tax policy disadvantage some while benefiting others? How does it support or undermine the economic security of individuals and families? How does it move responsibility for essential public services from one level of government to another, to families, or to the private sector? And does the overall tax system ultimately provide adequate revenue for the government to function at the level we need it to? Our examination of these issues can, in turn, suggest paths toward positive change that will improve the lives of all women and therefore their families, their communities, and the nation as a whole.

In framing this discussion, we have struggled with terms like "fair," "equitable," and "adequate." We've looked at the needs of women and the ultimate impact of current tax policy on individuals and society as a whole. Our goal is to bring more transparency to this complex and challenging issue, to illuminate the core values that must undergird our tax system, and to give our readers—especially women themselves—the tools to understand and participate in the ongoing debate on tax policy.

But we have also found that those debates are often misleading, that information broken down by gender and race is often missing, and that women's unique and diverse experiences are too often ignored. Many women's groups and fair tax organizations—including many members of the National Council for Research on Women—have offered important correctives. But their voices are too often drowned out or marginalized. This void has real implications for women—for their pocketbooks, for the services they receive, for the quality of life in their communities, and for their own futures and those of their children.

As a consortium of more than 100 research, policy, and advocacy organizations, the National Council for Research on Women is uniquely situated to help bring accurate information and new voices to the fore to address these complex issues. The Council's mission is to use the power of its network to ensure fully informed debate, policies, and practices, and build a more inclusive and equitable world for women and girls.

The genesis of *Taxes Are a Woman's Issue* was in the Council's Working Group on Economic Security. With 23 centers focused specifically on that issue, the Council brought together scholars and researchers, national advocates and grassroots activists, specialists in taxation, community development, and public policy to reframe questions, develop new strategies, and engage in broader debate on issues of pressing importance to women and girls. The Working Group drew on the work and insights of an even broader range of experts to help identify taxation from among many other issues as a topic of particular importance to women, whose special relationship to tax and spending policies were generally little understood and whose perspectives were generally lacking in public debate. An Advisory Committee, including the two primary authors, Mimi Abramovitz and Sandra Morgen, grew out of the Working Group to develop this volume. Research and consultations over one and a half years helped define the issues, develop new insights, identify the points of contention, and build new ways of thinking about tax policy and the ways it affects women. Finally a review process included an even broader range of readers—tax specialists, public policy experts and advocates, lay readers, economists, and specialists in other fields related to tax and spending policies.

The result is a volume that reflects a diversity of perspectives and expertise, one that acknowledges differences in approach and analyses, but one that draws on the points of consensus to begin to build an overarching understanding of tax and spending policies. It is also a call to action to our readers and to our nation's leaders to join those who are already working for a fair, adequate, and effective tax system. Specifically, we are asking our political leaders to consider the importance to women of a tax system based on one's ability to pay; to be mindful of the fundamental services that women need to ensure the well-being of their families; and to recall that tax-funded programs support the development of a healthy, educated, and globally competitive workforce. And because the playing field is not yet level, the government must collect and make available information that is disaggregated by gender, race, and other key variables so that the public can understand and address the different ways tax and spending policies affect all of our nation's people.

Finally, as the nation works its way through the contentious and complicated debate on tax policy and public spending, the Council calls on more women—and more women's research, policy, and advocacy organizations—to join those already taking action. Our appendix includes a list of some of the organizations already engaged in the struggle for change, and our website at *www.ncrw.org* will present additional information, new insights, and other resources as the debate unfolds. We hope this book helps ignite more interest, more understanding, and more action for a fair and just tax policy for all.

Linda Basch
President, National Council for Research on Women
December 2005

ACKNOWLEDGMENTS

The National Council for Research on Women would like to thank the following individuals and institutions for their generous financial support for this work:

> *The J.P. Morgan Chase Foundation*
> *Katherine M. Klotzburger*
> *Mariam Chamberlain*

We are also deeply grateful to the Ford Foundation for its general support of the Council during the life of this project.

Taxes Are a Woman's Issue represents the expertise, commitment, and vision of the National Council for Research on Women and its network of 106 research and policy centers. Led by its primary authors and guided by an expert Advisory Committee, the project has, from its inception to its completion, benefited from generous contributions of time and expertise from many people. It is a project that reflects the value and power of collaboration across all the differences of experience and perspective that the Council represents.

Primary throughout this project has been the support and encouragement of the Council;s Board of Directors Individually and as a group, they have helped guide the Council's overall work on economic security and contributed their insights and enthusiasm to this volume.

The authors, Mimi Abramovitz of the Hunter School of Social Work, City University of New York, and Sandra Morgen of the Center for the Study of Women in Society, University of Oregon, give special thanks to the staff of the Council, with whom they worked so closely over two years to bring this project to completion. Deputy Director Elizabeth Horton provided overall management of the project, helping with grace and persistence to tie together the additions of so many collaborators. Her commitment to this project was unflagging, and her contributions spanned the spectrum from writing and editing to oversight, and from deadline mistress to promoter of good humor. Gwendolyn Beetham, Research Associate, brought intelligence and diligence to basic research and fact-checking—a task that is, in a report like this, both a vital pursuit and a moving target. We are indebted to her for her professionalism, patience, and Holmesian skills. Deborah Siegel, Director of Special Projects and Member Relations, provided editorial support, helping to enliven the volume and make the complex issues covered in it more accessible. Anna Skiba-Crafts, Program and Executive Assistant, played a key role staffing the project from its first stages, providing additional research and editorial work as well as enthusiasm. Danielle Crowell, law student and Council intern, provided additional ongoing research on the Earned Income Tax Credit. Council President Linda Basch is owed our deepest gratitude for keeping the faith for a project that stretched out much longer than any of us imagined and that often took precious time from an overstretched staff. We also thank her for her substantive contributions to the report and for her commitment to making the Council a vital forum for bringing together research, public policy, and public dialogue.

For its part, the National Council for Research on Women wishes to thank Mimi Abramovitz and Sandra Morgen for their enormous contributions. As primary authors of the volume, they dedicated untold numbers of hours and lifetimes of knowledge and insight to the project. From the initial conceptualization through the innumerable revisions and additions to the final shaping of the report and its conclusions, they brought dedication, expertise, and an encompassing understanding of the larger issues involved in taxes and tax policy. We are grateful for their commitment to the issues raised in this volume, for their intellectual integrity, and for their great generosity of spirit. Without their outstanding work, this volume could not have been realized.

We owe deep gratitude to the many feminist scholars, policymakers, and allies from whom we sought guidance and ideas both early in this project and during the course of writing and editing the volume.

The initial impetus for this volume came from the work of the Council's Economic Security Working Group, made up of experts from the Council's network, which identified taxation as an issue of far-reaching importance to women. The Working Group is led by a Steering Committee chaired by Sandra Morgen and consisting of Mimi Abramovitz; Linda Basch; Mariam Chamberlain; Bonnie Thornton Dill, Director, Center for Race, Gender, and Ethnicity, University of Maryland, College Park; and Heidi Hartmann, President, Institute for Women's Policy Research.

A special Tax Advisory Committee read various drafts and provided critical input at key moments in the writing of the report. Members of the Committee include the Steering Committee as well as the following individuals: Eileen Appelbaum, Director of the Center for Women and Work, Rutgers University; Kathleen Barnett, Vice President, International Center for Research on Women; Linda Basch; Mariam Chamberlain; Bonnie Thornton Dill; Nancy Folbre, Professor of Economics, University of Massachusetts, Amherst; Heidi Hartmann; Alexandra Moses, Moses and Associates, P.C.; Heather Johnston Nicholson, Director of Research, Girls Incorporated; Lucie Lapovsky, economist and former President, Mercy College; Kathy Rodgers, President, Legal Momentum; Margaret Simms, Senior Vice President, Joint Center for Political and Economic Studies; Ronnie Steinberg, Director, Women's Social Policy & Research Center, Vanderbilt University; and Gale Summerfield, Director of the Women and Gender in Global Perspectives Program, University of Illinois at Urbana-Champaign.

We especially thank Heidi Hartmann and the members of her staff at the Institute for Women's Policy Research, including Avis Jones-DeWeever, Study Director for Poverty and Welfare, and Misha Werschkul, Mariam K. Chamberlain Fellow for several close readings and for deepening the analysis of Social Security policy included in the book, as well as many of the macroeconomic points throughout.

During the process of developing this volume, the Council consulted many other experts from its extended network of scholars and researchers, to whom we owe special thanks: Randy Albelda, Professor of Economics, University of Massachusetts, Boston; Sarita Bhalotra, Professor in the MBA and PhD programs at Brandeis University's Heller School; Heather Boushey, Economist, Center for Economic and Policy Research; Leslie Calman, Vice President of External Relations, International Center for Research on Women; Grace Chang, Professor of Women's Studies and Ethnic Studies; UC Santa Barbara and affiliated with the Center for Research on Women and Social Justice; Kaaryn Gustafson, Associate Professor of Law, University of Connecticut School of Law; Barbara Gault, Director of Research, Institute for Women's Policy Research; Elizabeth Gehl, Director of Public Policy, Business and Professional Women USA; Francine Moccio, Director of the Institute for Women and Work, Cornell University's School of Industrial and Labor Relations; Marilyn Moon, Vice President, American Institutes for Research; Dorothy Roberts, Professor at Northwestern Law School and Faculty Fellow at Northwestern's Institute for Policy Research; Donna Shavlik, The Timberline Group; Margaret Simms, Senior Vice President for Programs, Joint Center for Political and Economic Studies; Barbara Ellen Smith, Director of the Center for Research on Women, University of Memphis; Marie Wilson, President, The White House Project; and Ruth Zambrana, Graduate Director, Professor, and Director of Research at the Consortium on Race, Gender, and Ethnicity. University of Maryland, College Park.

Several experts from outside the orbit of Council member centers also reviewed drafts and provided new insights and clarifications: Dean Baker, Co-Director of the Center for Economic and Policy Research; Susan Berg, Adjunct Instructor, Hunter College School of Social Work; Iris Lav, Deputy Director at the Center on Budget and Policy Priorities; and Max Sawicky,

Economist at the Economic Policy Institute. We thank them all for sharing their expertise and helping to clarify the complex issues of taxation.

Sandra Morgen also extends thanks to staff and colleagues at the Center for the Study of Women in Society at the University of Oregon, who provided invaluable support during the writing of this book. Thanks especially to Shirley Marc, Priscilla Yamin, Jennifer Burton and Mara Fridell. She also wants to thank University of Oregon colleagues Margaret Hallock and Joan Acker for assistance and support. Additionally, two researchers/advocates from the Oregon Center for Public Policy—Chuck Sheketoff and Michael Leachman—have served as inspiration and have provided important insights about Oregon tax policy.

Mary Thom, writer and journalist, was a key member of the team, helping to shape and clarify complex issues and concepts. We thank her for her engagement, her intelligence, and the grace and power of her prose. We also extend our thanks to Vivian Todini, communications expert, for her advice and participation as we identified and refined the important messages of the volume.

We owe warm thanks to the seven women who contributed profiles to the text, each sharing their experiences and perspectives on how taxes *are* indeed a women's issue: Vickie Beetham, Avis Jones-DeWeever, Stephanie Lindquist, Guadalupe Quinn, Elyse Rudolph, Barbara Taft, and Shirley Williams-Johnson.

We also give special thanks to the experts and scholars who took the time to share with us their thoughts and perspectives on tax policy. Their contributions to the "Forum" at the end of the volume reflect the rich diversity of thinking related to taxes in the Council network and underscore the contributions women and the analysis of women's experience can make to the current debate on tax policy.

We express deep gratitude to the Feminist Press at the City University of New York, and particularly to Florence Howe, Executive Director, whose faith in the importance of this project carried us through its final phase and provided the encouragement necessary to transform the work into its current form. Jean Casella, former Publisher/Director of the Press, also deserves our gratitude for her help in initially conceptualizing the collaboration between the Press and the Council and for editing the volume with grace and sensitivity at the end of the process. We also send warm thanks to the full staff at the Feminist Press, who were instrumental in the final production of this book.

Finally, we are grateful to the member centers of the National Council for Research on Women, particularly the twenty-three centers represented in the resource guide to the book. We thank them for participating in this project and especially for the important work they do in providing information, insights, and new strategies to address the pressing issues of the day. Their research and analysis form the basis for much that is in this volume, as well as for our greater hopes for a fairer, more inclusive, and economically secure world for women and girls, their families, and their communities.

INTRODUCTION:
TRUTH AND TAXES

Women make up more than 50 percent of all taxpayers, and like all citizens, they have a major stake in an equitable and adequate tax system. But women also have a special interest in tax policy. As a group, they tend to shoulder similar responsibilities at home and in their communities, and face common issues in the workplace. And despite the great diversity among them—in race, age, ethnicity, and sexual orientation, and in marital, immigration, and economic status—women are generally disadvantaged by current tax and spending policies. For some, those policies merely compound inequities already built into our economy. For other women, they pose devastating threats to their fundamental security and that of their families. Together, these experiences reflect an inequality and injustice that is built into the ways the United States raises and spends the revenues necessary to fund essential public services. This injustice is both systemic and structural, affecting all women but not in the same ways or to the same degree. Understanding where various women have been well-served by the tax system as well as where they are disadvantaged can illuminate the ways our public tax and spending policies impact all people.

HOW ARE WOMEN AFFECTED BY TAX POLICY?

Women, of course, reflect the full diversity of our society. But they do share a certain relationship to taxes and tax policy.

- Women tend to earn less on average than men, so they benefit from a progressive tax system that taxes people according to their ability to pay, unlike a flat, or regressive, tax system.
- Women's income is more likely to come disproportionately from wages rather than from dividends or other income from wealth, so they are unfairly penalized when wages are taxed more heavily than income from wealth.
- Women tend to be more responsible for care-giving in the family, which means they often rely more on public services like health care and dependent care.
- Women are more likely than men to work part-time, interrupt their work lives, and spend fewer years in the paid labor force. They thus have less access to employer-provided benefits and a greater need for tax-supported services like income security programs and health insurance.
- Women are more often single parents, so they rely more heavily on tax-funded prenatal care, income support, child-care, and education.
- Women tend to live longer than men, so they need good retirement benefits, including health coverage. But because women often work in the paid economy for fewer years and at lower wages than men, they rely more on Social Security and other publicly funded benefits for the elderly.
- Finally, women are now almost half of all wage earners, but the tax system was formed before they entered the workforce in great numbers—and their changing roles in the paid economy have not been taken into consideration as the system has evolved.

Women, then, as a group occupy a certain position in our society and our economy—a position that places them at the center of conflicts over how we, as a nation, tax ourselves, and how we spend that tax money.

UNDERSTANDING THE ISSUES, REFRAMING THE DEBATE

Public policy debates typically marginalize women's experiences. Very little published tax information is broken down by gender, race, or ethnicity. Information about women as taxpayers, the tax contribution of wives, the tax benefits received by women, or many other gender-related details are generally not available.

Information that is not missing is often misleading. Those who are most well-grounded in tax policy tend to see it through a narrow focus, often limited to the ever-changing technical minutiae of tax laws or as defined by political ideology. We certainly don't get an accurate picture from most politicians, who often substitute sound bytes and rhetoric for serious discussions about government tax and spending decisions. Nor do the media usually provide the kind of analysis of tax policy that sheds light on the underlying issues or the real impact of current policies on individuals.

The language often used to frame debates about tax policy adds to the confusion. Terms like "tax relief," "tax reform," and "local control" have been used to garner support for tax cuts that overwhelmingly favor high-income individuals and large corporations. The rhetoric of the tax "burden" has been used to undermine our understanding of the reciprocal relationship between taxpayers and governments that provide the public services essential to our national well-being. And anti-tax activists who rail against "tax and spend" policies have used the rhetoric to deflect attention from a long overdue dialogue about an adequate and effective level of public services, ignoring the fact that a policy based on taxing fairly and spending wisely is always a sound public policy.

Without good, accurate data, scholars and policymakers don't have the tools to analyze tax policies or design fair and viable tax systems. Without informed analysis, advocates and citizens can't assess the impact of changes in tax policy on their own personal situations. Without clear and honest language, we are unable as a nation to engage in meaningful debate about the mounting stress on both individual taxpayers and government budgets. And without a fundamental faith in the fairness of the tax system and the adequacy of public services, taxpayers are increasingly unwilling to see beyond their own immediate self-interest to the long-term greater good of the community and society at large.

TAXES *ARE* A WOMAN'S ISSUE

With recent changes in national tax policy, with increasing strains on governmental budgets, and with a polarized public debate about taxes swirling in the media, we cannot afford to leave the issues of taxation to specialists, lobbyists, and ideologues. We all need to understand the ways tax policies undergird our national well-being and reflect our national values. We need to understand how the structure of taxes and our complex system of tax deductions, exemptions, and credits either promote or undercut the economic security of individuals and families. We need to understand the direct connection between taxes and the public services that are so important to all of us, to our families, our businesses, and our communities. We need to reframe the debate, away from the technical discussions of tax code and the limited perspectives driven by ideology or self-interest, and toward tax literacy and real tax reform. And we need to ask the fundamental question of how we can best use tax policy to mitigate the deepening economic inequality that characterizes our society today.

The goal of this volume is to demystify the tax system, to bring women into the debate, and to foster a new kind of tax literacy, one that includes a deeper knowledge of the impact of tax policy on the lives of all women, their families, and their communities. It offers an introduction to tax policy for those who find the subject mysterious and daunting. But it also provides a new, more inclusive perspective on taxes and government spending for those already well-grounded in taxation. It uses women's diverse experiences to reframe the issues related to taxation and provides a new canvas for analyzing and understanding the ways our system impact all taxpayers. It includes women's voices, so often underrepresented in debates on tax policy, to help bring fresh ideas and strategies for real reform that will benefit everyone. Finally, it provides readers with some of the tools they need both to participate in public debate and to advocate for a fairer, more progressive tax system. For women in particular, this means a system of tax and spending priorities that takes women's work experience—paid and unpaid—into account and provides adequate public resources for the services needed by women, their families, and communities.

This book is a call to bring women's voices and experiences to the debate about taxation. It is a call to all citizens to understand and help reframe the discussion, to advocate for fair, effective tax policy. With basic definitions and reliable information, with analysis from experts and profiles of individual women taxpayers, and with a broad view of the ways tax and spending policies play out for women, this volume will help different readers understand and talk about taxes in new and clear ways.

Since this book is meant as both an introduction to taxation and a reframing of the issue for those who need new and broader perspectives, we encourage different readers to use the information in the following chapters in different ways. The organization of the book allows readers to navigate it for themselves, moving quickly or more slowly through it, focusing on the insights that are most relevant.

Chapter 1, "Who Are Women Taxpayers and What Do They Need to Know?" gives a brief portrait of women across social, economic, racial, and generational divides. It shows the differences in their experiences as well as the commonalities. It also lays out the seven basic points that all women need to know about tax policy.

Chapter 2, "Tax Talk 101," is a primer for those who would like a basic introduction. It defines terms used throughout the volume and gives a conceptual overview of tax policy, including the ways taxes are structured and their relationship to broader social, political, and economic issues.

Chapter 3, "Women and Taxes," analyzes the dual "welfare" system that includes social welfare (direct spending on programs for individuals and families) and fiscal welfare (tax credits, exemptions, and deductions that are part of the tax code). Both systems address the same basic needs, and tax revenues fund both. However, the former is especially important to women, but often under attack from anti-tax, small-government advocates, while the latter, which benefits taxpayers at all income levels, but especially those who are more well-off, is often unnoticed, unanalyzed, and unchallenged in current debates on tax and spending policies.

Chapter 4, "How We Got Here," looks at the history of U.S. tax policies, and particularly how the declining progressivity of those policies over the last 30 years has harmed women. It tracks the ways in which tax policies have reflected evolving views of the role of government and changing economic theories, disadvantaging those at the bottom of the income scale, including a disproportionate number women.

Chapter 5, "How Today's Policies Hurt Women, Children, and Families," analyzes the impact of current tax policies on the economy as a whole through the experiences of women. It looks at recent changes in the federal income tax, the growth of payroll taxes, and the decrease in the relative levels of taxation on corporate profits and wealth. It examines the consequences of those changes, particularly the growing gap between the rich and the poor and the increasing squeeze on public services.

Chapter 6, "Why Women Feel More Sting from Service Cuts," follows the prior chapter with an analysis of how that squeeze on public services is playing out in the areas that are especially important to women and their families.

Each of the first six chapters ends with "Straight Talk About Taxes," summing up the major points of the chapter and providing talking points for discussion. Threaded throughout the volume are profiles of seven individual women, each differently situated in relation to taxes, to put human faces to this diversity.

Chapter 7, "Real Women Need Real Tax Reform," lays out some of the principles we believe real tax reform should address. It poses questions all citizens can ask when thinking through proposed policy changes and identifies specific policy decisions we feel all women can support, both for the short run and in the long term.

The books ends with a special section, "Forum: Views from the Council's Network of Centers," which provides a rich compendium of some of the current thinking on tax policy, by experts in their own voices from the Council's network.

An appendix following the text of the book includes more resources and information about organizations working for real tax reform, and another provides a full list of National Council for Research on Women member centers.

1 | WHO ARE WOMEN TAXPAYERS AND WHAT DO THEY NEED TO KNOW?

Taxes are probably the most important thing that women should be thinking about. They're not dull, they're not incomprehensible, and they are not the root of all evil. They are the root of every policy decision our government makes.

—*Kathy Rodgers, President, Legal Momentum*

WHAT MAKES WOMEN TAXPAYERS DIFFERENT?

Just as there is no generic taxpayer, there is no generic woman taxpayer. Our tax bills differ based on the amount and sources of our income and the makeup of our households. But historically, most women have shared certain traits in relationship to tax and spending policies. And that relationship has changed in recent decades, as more women become breadwinners and family patterns have altered. So who are today's women taxpayers? How do they differ from male taxpayers? And what are the similarities and differences among women taxpayers?

Women earn less than men. In 1999, women constituted 49 percent of all federal income taxpayers, but on average they earned only 57 percent of what men earned.[1] This is true for women at all income levels because they are more likely than men to work part-time, because they tend to hold lower paying jobs, and because they are often paid less for comparable work.

In 2003, for example, while women were 48 percent of the workforce, they were 61 percent of the minimum wage earners.[2] The Institute for Women's Policy Research (IWPR) reports that 42 percent of men earn more than $50,000 annually, while only 9 percent of women reach that salary level.[3] Even as they reach managerial positions, women are paid less than men. A recent study by the U.S. government's General Accounting Office found that women managers earned less than their male counterparts in the ten industries that employ the majority of women. In 2000, women earned on average 77 cents for every dollar earned by their male counterparts. Between 1995 and 2000, according to the GAO, that gap actually widened in seven of the industries studied (even after controlling for age, marital status, and race).[4]

There are other signs that the earning gap between women and men is not going away. In 2003, according to Census Bureau data, the median earnings for full-time, year-round women workers fell from $30,895 in 2002 to $30,724. Comparable earnings for men remained essentially unchanged at $40,668. Women in the workforce full-time that year earned 76 percent of what men earned, compared to 77 percent the previous year.[5] Accounting for other factors that affect women's income over the long term, such as their need to work part-time or interrupt their careers to care for families, the earnings gap widens considerably; the Institute for Women's Policy Research reports that over the course of a fifteen-year study, women in the prime of their work lives earned only 38 percent of what men earned.[6]

Women tend to be clustered in lower income groups. In 2003, women constituted 63 percent of those in the lowest fifth on the income scale, where the average income is $8,201, and 55 percent of those in the second-lowest fifth, with an average income of $21,478. They made up only 41 percent of those in the highest fifth, where incomes averaged $127,146. (See graph 1.1) In 2004, median annual earnings for all women, including those who work part time, declined for the fourth year in a row, to an average of $22,200.[7]

GRAPH 1.1
WHERE WOMEN STAND ON THE INCOME SCALE, 2003

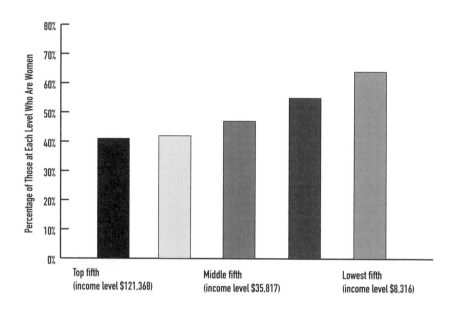

Source: U.S. Department of Labor, Bureau of Labor Statistics (2003), *Consumer Expenditure Survey 2003*, Table 55: Quintiles of income before taxes: Shares of aggregate expenditures and sources of income: <http://www.bls.gov/cex/2003/aggregate/quintile.pdf>.

Women are less likely to have a financial cushion. Continued pay inequity, along with more frequently interrupted work patterns, also means that women, especially single women, are more likely to live paycheck-to-paycheck throughout their work lives, with less in savings for current needs and lower pensions later in life. For example, while 28 percent of all Americans—both men and women—recently reported spending all of their earnings every month,[8] more of younger, single women (53 percent) said they were living paycheck-to-paycheck than did younger, single men (42 percent).[9] Younger, single women (ages 25 to 34) also spent a larger percent of their yearly after-tax income—99 percent, compared with 88 percent for men.[10] Women are thus more likely to need social safety net programs in times of personal crisis or economic downturn. As they age, a greater percentage of women are single compared to men, making them more dependent on a single paycheck for income and savings—and more vulnerable to catastrophic events like job loss or severe illness. Sixty percent of older women in America today are single (whether as a result of divorce, widowhood, or never being married), compared with 23.5 percent of men.[11]

Women's earnings vary according to race. Women are racially and ethnically diverse, reflecting the diversity of the nation. (See graph 1.2.) White and Asian American women continue to earn considerably more, on average, than African American and Hispanic women—as do their male counterparts. (See graph 1.3.) (While Native American women are not included in this graph, statistics from earlier years show the earnings of Native American women as lower than all but Hispanic women.)

GRAPH 1.2
RACE AND ETHNICITY OF U.S. WOMEN, 2000

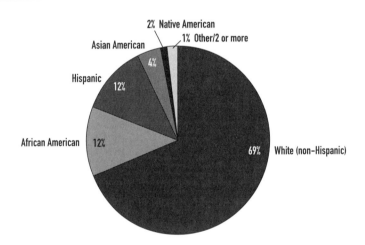

Source: Misha Werschkul and Erica Williams (2004), *The Status of Women in the States*, Appendix Table 1, Institute for Women's Policy Research: <http://www.iwpr.org/States2004/PDFs/National.pdf>.

GRAPH 1.3
EARNINGS DIFFERENCES AMONG WOMEN, BY RACE AND ETHNICITY, 2003

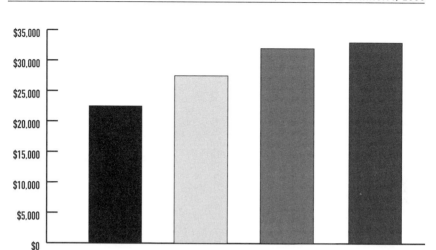

Source: Institute for Women's Policy Research (2005), *African American Women Work More, Earn Less* (29 March): <http://www.iwpr.org/pdf/IWPRRelease3_29_05.pdf>.

Women's poverty rates are higher than men's. Women have long been more likely than men to live below the poverty level. And since 2001, the number of women living in poverty has risen steadily. In 2004, 12.7 percent—or 14.3 million women—were living in poverty, compared with 9.3 percent of men.[12] Poverty rates also differ by race: they are twice as high for African American women and Latinas as they are for White women.[13] (See graph 1.4.)

GRAPH 1.4
POVERTY RATES AMONG U.S. WOMEN, 2003

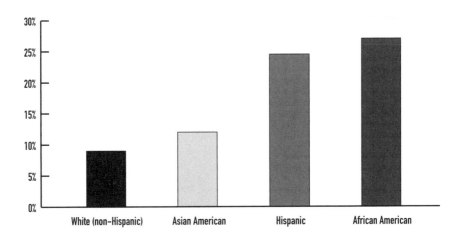

Source: Institute for Women's Policy Research (2005), *African American Women Work More, Earn Less* (March 29): <http://www.iwpr.org/pdf/IWPRRelease3_29_05.pdf>.

Women's taxes are dramatically affected by family status. All taxpayers' tax status is determined, in part, on whether they are married, single, or the head of a household with dependents. But family status affects women and men's tax status in different ways. Only about half of women in the United States are married. (See graph 1.5.) Just over half of all U.S. households include married couples,[14] and a minority of those are "traditional" households headed by one—male—wage earner. In 1999, 60 percent of joint tax returns included two earners. But 75 percent of those filings showed men earning 50 percent or more of the total reported income from wages and salaries.[15]

At the same time, 52 percent of wage earners who filed individually rather than jointly were women.[16] In general, women-headed households have about one-half the income and less than one-third the wealth of other U.S. households.[17] Almost 21 percent of families with children under 18 are headed by women,[18] although this varies substantially according to racial and ethnic background. In 2000, about 50 percent of African American, 30 percent of Native American, 22 percent of Hispanic, 16 percent of White, and 10 percent of Asian American families with children under 18 were headed by women.[19]

GRAPH 1.5
MARITAL STATUS OF U.S. WOMEN AGED 15 AND OLDER, 2000

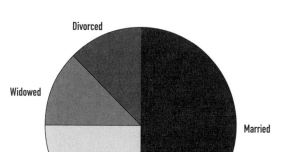

Source: Misha Werkschul and Erica Williams (2004), *The Status of Women in the States*, Appendix Table 3, Institute for Women's Policy Research: <http://www.iwpr.org/States2004/PDFs/National.pdf>.

Other variables also affect women as taxpayers. These factors include age, sexual orientation, (dis)ability level, and immigration status.

In 2000, approximately 1,342,000 households were headed by women 15 to 24 years old; this comprised 10.5 percent of all female-headed households. Young women and girls are an active part of the economy as spenders. Girls and young women eight to 21 years of age account for approximately $41 billion in sales, much of it subject to sales tax.[20] They are also significant wage earners: annual earnings of employed teens exceed $85 billion.[21] Young women at the age of fourteen are slightly more likely than their male counterparts to work, but by age fifteen, the rates of employment are essentially the same.[22]

Lesbian households numbered 326,066 in 2000 according to Census Bureau data, although the data are incomplete.[23] Information about lesbians is often conflated with data about gay men, who typically earn more than lesbians. But recent data suggests that coupled lesbians earn more than other women but less than heterosexual couple households. The poverty rate of same-sex households stood at 5 percent in 2000, about half the national poverty rate.[24]

Twenty-eight million U.S. women are living with disabilities.[25] The rate of disability is higher for women than it is for men in nearly all racial and ethnic categories.[26] Of the 24.3 million women who receive some type of Social Security benefits, slightly more than 10 percent of them receive disability benefits as workers.[27] African American women are twice as likely as White women to receive disability benefits, and women of other races (including Asian Pacific Islanders, American Indians, and Alaska Natives) are three times as likely.[28] Women also receive lower levels of disability benefits. In 2003, women on disability received, on average, $734.40 monthly, while men received $965.90.[29] Women with work-related disabilities also experience higher poverty rates—about 34 percent, as compared with 24 percent for men with work-related disabilities.[30]

Immigrant women are 10.9 percent of the total female population. In 2003, the real median income of foreign-born households was $37,499 compared with $47,347 for native-born households, and their poverty rates were higher as well—17.2 percent for the foreign-born versus 11.8 percent for the native-born.[31] Immigrants pay income, payroll, and sales taxes, but a variety of federal and state laws make them ineligible for many forms of public assistance. The estimated 6 million undocumented immigrant workers (about 5 percent of the U.S. workforce) who pay Social Security, income, and other taxes do not qualify for benefits at all, except in extreme circumstances.[32] Even undocumented workers with official Individual Taxpayer Identification Numbers, which allow them to file tax returns, are not eligible for benefits like the Earned Income Tax Credit when they submit their returns.

Finally, women business owners make up a growing proportion of the self-employed—another factor affecting tax status. In 1975, women were one of every four self-employed workers, but by the century's end, they constituted 40 percent of self-employed workers.[33] However, according to the Small Business Administration, 87 percent of businesses owned by women earn under $50,000 annually. These businesses tend to be small, and located in economic sectors that have lower incomes, such as beauty parlors, small specialty shops, catering services, and child-care.

In sum, while women are broadly diverse and experience tax and spending policies according to their individual circumstances, they also share a common position within our society and within our economy. In order to understand how tax policy affects each woman individually, we must see how it affects women as a group. In order to act and advocate for real tax reform, we must see some of the underlying structures that affect all women, and we must understand some of the principles that serve all of us well, despite our individual differences.

WHAT EVERY WOMAN NEEDS TO KNOW ABOUT TAXES

We need taxes. Some conservative economic theorists like to suggest that the market can address the nation's needs without government intervention. In practice, however, we need government services to regulate currency, patents, international trade, and other functions on which the market depends. We also depend on the government for clean air, safe streets, disaster relief, adequate wages for all, a safety net for the needy, and other necessities that private companies do not necessarily provide while making a profit. Nor is the market always able to allocate costs to individual users and collect the money for those services we use collectively, like national defense and environmental protection. The private sector also will not deliver goods and services that are important to the well-being of the whole community, like education, to those who cannot pay. So the government steps in by raising tax revenues to support needed government services, by offering incentives to the private sector to produce those goods and services, and by creating programs to help individuals and communities marginalized or excluded by the market.

We all benefit from tax-supported programs. Taxes represent our collective investment in the society as a whole. While anti-tax activists often focus the tax debate on spending for social programs for the poor, we all benefit from tax-funded programs that range from interstate highways, public education, and police protection to Social Security, national security, health services, and safety net programs. A second, less visible set of benefits consists of tax deductions, exemptions, and credits—such as deductions for mortgage interest payments, the cost of raising children, and medical and retirement savings accounts. Referred to in this book as "fiscal welfare," these tax benefits represent another way to support our common and individual needs. Together these two ways of providing public support serve all income groups, and people of all races, ages, religions, and ethnicities.

Women play multiple roles in the tax system. Like men, women participate in the tax system on four main fronts: as taxpayers who contribute to the nation's income, as consumers of the public goods and services funded by their hard-earned tax dollars, as employees in the public sector that produces these goods and services, and as citizens who participate in debate and decision making about tax policy.

Taxes affect different women in different ways. Tax policy does not affect all women in the same way. A woman's class, race, ethnicity, age, sexual orientation, marital status, immigration status, employment history, family structure, income, and wealth influence how much she pays in taxes, what proportion of her household income is left after taxes, and which tax-funded public services she needs and can access. The tax bills for three women with the same income—one married, one single, and the third a single head-of-household—vary to reflect their different economic status. However, in some cases, our tax system does not account for important differences. For example, low-wage women—a group disproportionately comprised of women of color—are hit especially hard by "flat" taxes like state and local sales taxes. Because these taxes do not take into account one's ability to pay, they have a disproportionate impact on the ability of low-income earners to cover their living expenses; in effect, they are regressive taxes.

A progressive system is becoming less so. Since the end of World War II, the overall tax system in the United States has become less progressive. Based on the principle of taxing people according to their ability to pay, a progressive tax increases the rate of taxation as one's income rises. Progressive tax systems take more from those with more, thus ensuring enough government revenue and allowing those whose household incomes are less robust to retain more of their income to cover basic needs. Over the last fifty years, the overall tax system has shifted gradually, moving the balance away from taxes on wealth toward taxes on wages, away from the progressive income tax to increasing dependence on state and local sales taxes and other less progressive forms of taxation. Changes to the tax code since 2001—including lower income tax rates for the highest earners, reductions in the estate and capital gains taxes, and new tax deductions and exemptions—have dramatically accelerated this trend. Sold as a benefit for the middle class,[34] these changes have instead mainly favored corporations and the top income groups. Since women generally earn lower salaries than men, rely more on wages than on dividends or other income from wealth, and more often have interrupted career patterns, they tend to be particularly disadvantaged as the system relies less and less on progressive taxes.

Less is not more. Recent changes to the tax system are contributing to reduced public revenues. This, along with large increases in military, homeland security, and disaster relief spending, is helping to drain the U.S. Treasury, enlarge the federal budget deficit, and raise the national debt. To pay its bills, the government has borrowed heavily and placed essential but already seriously underfunded programs—including education, health, and housing programs—in jeopardy. For a number of reasons, these cuts particularly affect women.

As care providers, women still carry out a disproportionate share of domestic work, even when they also work outside the home. When tax cuts lead to cuts in programs that directly or indirectly support care work—like income support, subsidized child-care, or nursing homes for Alzheimer's patients—the costs and burdens of caring for families and communities shift from the general society onto the shoulders of women, affecting their capacity to work outside the home and the overall quality of their lives.

As consumers, women represent the majority of participants in safety net and entitlement programs. Because they live longer, they are the majority of Social Security and Medicare recipients. Because they are more often single parents, they rely more on Temporary Aid to Needy Families (TANF). Because they more often serve as care-givers in families, they are the majority of people who need to use child-care, elder-care, and other care-giving services. Because they are more likely to depend on such services, government-supported domestic violence prevention and family planning programs are especially important to women. For poor women and those with middle and low incomes who rely on these programs, tax cuts translate into service cuts.

As public sector employees, women outnumber men, with 18 percent of women employed in public jobs, compared with 13 percent of men.[35] Women are also the majority of employees in institutions funded by tax dollars. For example, in 2003, women were 80.6 percent of all elementary and middle school teachers and 90.2 percent of all registered nurses.[36] For these women, tax and spending cuts translate into job cuts.

In brief, many government programs serve women well. Access to government services can increase women's economic independence, provide them with greater "bargaining power" at home and on the job, and help expand their life choices. While this economic backup is meaningful to all women, it is especially important to single mothers; to women caring for elderly parents; to victims of discrimination or domestic violence; to women trying to balance all of their responsibilities in the workplace, in families, and in communities

Real women need real tax reform. The tax system is opaque. Average taxpayers find it difficult to negotiate without tax services or accountants. The system's complexities also blur who gains—and who does not—from a particular policy. But many policies recently advanced under the banner of "tax reform" are really aimed at reducing taxes—and most often, at reducing taxes on wealth.

We do not need to trade fairness and adequacy for a simple tax system. Everyone, especially women, would profit immeasurably from thoughtful, transparent reforms of government tax policy that make the system easier to understand. However, too few women are in public policy decision-making positions, and many women voters do not fully understand the profound ramifications of tax policies on themselves and on society.

STRAIGHT TALK ABOUT WOMEN AND TAXES: HOW TO MAKE THE CASE

To those who say: Taxes are not a woman's issue—they're everyone's issue.

We say: Yes, taxes are everyone's issue, but women are affected in unique and diverse ways—and their experiences are often not taken into consideration when tax policy is discussed. While women are more than half of all taxpayers, the overall U.S. tax system evolved based on the model of the one-earner, male breadwinner family, and consequently fails to support the different ways in which women now take on paid and unpaid labor.

- Women earn less than men, more often work part-time jobs, and are more likely to have interrupted careers. Therefore, regressive taxes, which leave even less in their pockets after taxes, hit women particularly hard.
- These work patterns also mean that women tend to have fewer work-related benefits, like health insurance and retirement benefits, leaving them more reliant on publicly provided services.
- Women are poorer and bear much of the almost invisible burden of caregiving in our society. They are also more likely to be single parents. Therefore, tax-supported programs like child-care assistance and Temporary Aid to Needy Families (TANF) have special importance in helping them balance work and family obligations and in providing some level of income security.
- Women live longer than men and have fewer private retirement funds. They therefore depend more on Social Security, Medicare, and other services for the elderly.
- Women are underrepresented at the decision-making table. In 2005, they comprise only 15 percent of the people serving in the U.S. Congress, and also lack parity at other levels of public policy leadership.

2 | TAX TALK 101: WHAT GETS TAXED, WHY, AND HOW

In recent decades, talk about tax policy has shifted away from the very real fact that taxes support a representative democracy—taxes pay for the society in which we all live, for our schools, our roads, and to pick up our garbage. Tax-literate women will be able to re-educate the public and reframe the debate back to one which recognizes the importance of taxes to a well-functioning democracy.

—Marie Wilson, President, The White House Project and Founder,
Take Our Daughters to Work Day

WHAT'S A TAX?

A tax is a way of transferring money from individuals or businesses, typically based on their income, property, or other wealth, to support government services. Federal and local governments also raise revenues through general sales taxes, specialized excise taxes on specific products, import tariffs, and fees for services like marriage licenses and phone service.[1] Some of these, like income taxes, we pay directly; others are imbedded in the cost of goods and services; and still others target the users of particular public services rather than the general public.

WHAT GETS TAXED?

We all pay more than one kind of tax. The federal government and some states and localities levy a tax on *personal incomes*, including wage and interest earnings, and other forms of income. It taxes individual investors on *capital gains*—earnings from profits on the sale of stocks and real estate. At the death of someone with a large estate, heirs may pay federal and possibly state *estate taxes* or *inheritance taxes*. Businesses pay *corporate taxes* on their profits. States and many cities impose *consumption taxes* or *sales taxes*, a percentage of the price consumers pay for certain goods and services. Governments also levy special sales taxes called *excise taxes* on certain goods such as fuel, alcoholic beverages, and luxury items. *User fees* support highways, airports, telephone services, and much more. The *payroll tax* (automatically deducted from employees' paychecks) supports Social Security, Medicare, and disability benefits. Finally, both individuals and businesses pay state or local *property taxes* on real estate and on such property as boats, automobiles, and business inventories.[2]

WHY DO WE NEED TAXES?

No one enjoys giving up hard-earned dollars, and reasonable people may disagree about funding priorities. Yet almost everyone recognizes that tax-supported government services play a key role in society. They help ensure the smooth functioning of our society by providing needed goods and services and by promoting economic growth and political stability. For example, tax-funded programs provide stable currency; trade, patent, and copyright laws; and other functions necessary to support the private sector; ensure public order and security; supply business with a healthy, educated, and productive workforce; mitigate the personal suffering and ease the social discontent that can result when the basic needs of people go unmet; and underwrite the cost of care-giving work, which is of special importance to women.

Despite our individual and collective need for the services that taxes fund, anti-tax advocates try to cast taxes as an unreasonable burden, as "stealing money from people's pockets." The Tax Foundation and other anti-tax activists even celebrate Tax Freedom Day, "the day when Americans will finally have earned enough money to pay off their total tax bill for the year."[3] Their message is clear: taxes are a burden from which we need to be freed.

In contrast, economist Nancy Folbre talks about our "tax payback age," the year that each of us has finally paid back in taxes the cost of all the government services we use in a lifetime. These include the tax deductions provided to our parents the day we were born, the cost for most of us of our public education, the fire and police protection we enjoy in our town and cities, the support we receive to raise and educate our own children, and ultimately our retirement and health benefits.[4]

WHAT DO TAXES PAY FOR?

Different states and different localities allocate their tax revenues differently. But we all pay federal taxes, and we all need to know where our federal taxes go. In 2005, federal taxes were budgeted at roughly $2,036,000,000,000 (that's 2 trillion 36 billion dollars[5]). Graph 2.1 shows how our money was spent in Fiscal Year 2004. Graph 2.2 shows where that money came from.

GRAPH 2.1
FEDERAL SPENDING, FY 2004

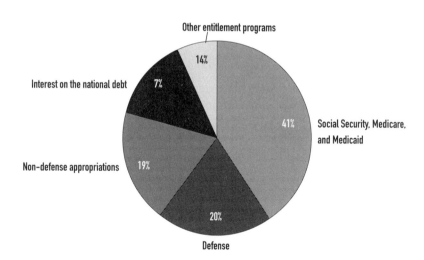

Other entitlement programs 14%

Interest on the national debt 7%

Social Security, Medicare, and Medicaid 41%

Non-defense appropriations 19%

Defense 20%

Source: Martha Cogan and Richard Koven (2004), *Introduction to the Federal Budget Process* (December 29), Center on Budget and Policy Priorities: <http://www.cbpp.org/3-7-03bud.htm>.

GRAPH 2.2
FINANCING THE BUDGET, FY 2004

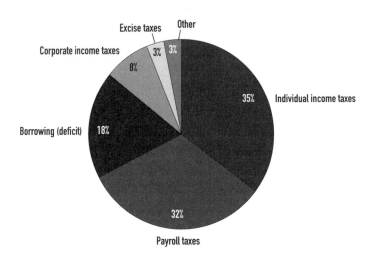

Source: Martha Cogan and Richard Koven (2004), *Introduction to the Federal Budget Process* (December 29), Center on Budget and Policy Priorities: <http://www.cbpp.org/3-7-03bud.htm>.

Public expenditures can be categorized into two broad groupings.

Public Infrastructure and Services. Tax dollars fund basic services, infrastructures, and amenities that support our economy, protect our civil society, and improve the quality of life for all of us—public schools and courts, libraries and colleges, trains and buses, highways and bridges, police, fire, and emergency protection, forests and parks, scientific research, airport and road safety, and clean food, air, and water. Tax revenues provide price supports to some farmers, protect some U.S. firms from foreign imports, bail out failing corporations, and support the profits of business and industry directly with subsidies and indirectly through tax benefits. A large proportion of our tax revenue pays for national defense. Another hefty chunk goes to pay interest on our national debt. Tax-funded programs also ensure that individuals and families have access to a range of services at various points in the life cycle, such as public education for children and adolescents, child-care for working parents, and health care for the elderly.[6]

Both individual well-being and business profits depend on these essential services. Using tax revenues, governments must either produce the goods or services themselves or fund nonprofit organizations, and, increasingly, for-profit companies, to deliver them.

The Social Safety Net. Historically, and especially since the Great Depression, tax revenues have helped ensure a basic level of support for many citizens. While race discrimination and exclusion from social welfare programs meant that originally most people of color did not benefit from that support, by the 1960s most of the population did have access, at least to some degree, thanks to the work of civil rights and welfare rights activists. Disabilities, low wages, lack of education and employment opportunities, race and sex discrimination—and times of severe economic downturn—mean that many people lack the money needed to buy basic goods and services. Given this reality, most industrial nations tax those with the ability to pay in order to help people with the most pressing needs: those who cannot find jobs or are too old, young, sick, or disabled to provide for themselves.

When these safety net programs are threatened, women are especially affected. They are more likely to have limited incomes, to have smaller pensions, and to live longer. Regardless of race, class, or ethnicity, it is women—single mothers, married housewives, working women, daughters of aging parents, public sector workers—who disproportionately care for those who rely on others for care. They are often the silent shock absorbers when family problems arise, when communities undergo crises, and when the economy sags. However meagerly, government benefits reduce poverty among the elderly, underwrite the cost of women's unpaid carework in the home, ease the pressure of economic insecurity, and help women balance work and family responsibilities.

A *Personal Story:* Protect Public Services!

Elyse Rudolph is the White, upper-middle-class executive director of the Literacy Assistance Center, a nonprofit that focuses on adult education in New York City. She commutes every day from her home in New Jersey, where she lives with her husband and two school-age daughters.

Have recent tax cuts helped her? Well, yes, she says. With her own $100,000-plus income as well as her husband's income, the family did receive a substantial break on their federal taxes—and thanks to New York State's repeal of the commuter tax, she no longer pays any taxes to New York City where she works.

Is she happy about those tax cuts? Definitely not! As she says, "I work in the shadow of what was the World Trade Center. On 9/11, I depended on public services for my safety and that of my staff. And I want to know that those services—as well as the school my daughters go to and the public road and transportation system I rely on—will be there for me and for all of us when we need them." In addition, the federal tax cuts have brought financial tradeoffs—like ballooning property taxes on the family's New Jersey home.

But it's the impact on adult learners, and the programs that serve them, that brings real passion to Rudolph's voice. President Bush's 2006 budget proposal included a cut of 66 percent in the Workforce Investment Title II dollars, which fund almost half of her agency's work, as well as that of most other literacy programs across the nation. Rudolph points to the devastation this level of cuts would mean—to individuals and to society as a whole. "Literacy programs are the most significant route toward self-reliance for millions of individuals and their families. Those programs build our workforce, ensure the quality of our civic life, and help break the generational cycle of illiteracy, dependency, and poverty."

The bottom line: "They can keep those tax breaks—I want enough public money to fund the essential public services we all need and want!"

HOW ARE TAXES STRUCTURED?

Even Adam Smith, the eighteenth-century thinker long considered the progenitor of free market economics, recognized the wisdom of a progressive tax system. In his famous 1776 treatise *The Wealth of Nations*, Smith wrote:

> The subjects of every state ought to contribute toward the support of the government, as nearly as possible, in proportion to their respective abilities; that is, in proportion to the revenue which they respectively enjoy under the protection of the state . . . [a goal of taxation should be to] remedy inequality of riches as much as possible, by relieving the poor and burdening the rich.[7]

The U.S. tax system includes two main types of taxes: progressive (graduated) taxes, which are designed so that the tax rate, or the percentage of income taken in taxes, increases as the taxpayer's income increases, and proportional or regressive taxes, which take the same or an even greater proportion from low-income taxpayers than from the wealthy. The use of these different tax structures determines how the tax bill is distributed: who pays how much of the cost of vital government services, and how much after-tax money remains for each household to pay for basic needs, save for the future, and spend on other goods and services.

Progressive Taxes. A progressive tax structure reflects society's commitment to the principle that contributions to the cost of government should be based on one's ability to pay and that taxpayers with similar incomes should pay similar levels of taxes. Progressive taxes leave those with low incomes with a larger share of their income after taxes to pay their basic expenses. They take more from those who have adequate after-tax income for their needs. A progressive tax divides income into a number of brackets with specified cutoff values, and assigns a higher tax rate to the income in each bracket as the dollar value of the bracket rises. For example, the current U.S. federal income tax code is progressive in that the percentage taken from higher income brackets is greater than that taken from lower ones. (See table 2.1.)

TABLE 2.1
2004 U.S. TAX RATES FOR SINGLE PERSON FILING

Taxable income	Marginal Tax Rates
$0–$7,150	**10 percent** of the amount over $0
$7,150–$29,050	$715 plus **15 percent** of the amount over $7,150
$29,050–$70,350	$4,000 plus **25 percent** of the amount over 29,050
$70,350–$146,750	$14,325 plus **28 percent** of the amount over 70,350
$146,750–$319,100	$35,717 plus **33 percent** of the amount over $146,750
$319,100–no limit	$92,592.50 plus **35 percent** of the amount over $319,100

Source: U.S. Internal Revenue Service (2004), *Tax Rate Schedules*: <http://www.irs.gov/formspubs/article/0,,id=133625,00.html>.

A taxpayer's *marginal tax rate* is the rate applied to income that falls within a specific bracket. For example, if a taxpayer earned $25,000 a year, her taxable income would be $17,050 after subtraction of the $3,100 personal exemption and $4,850 standard deduction for a single person. She would pay a 10 percent *marginal rate* on the first $10,000 of income and an additional 15 percent on the next $7,050. Her tax bill would total $2,058, assuming she had no special deductions or credits. The *average tax rate* or *effective tax rate* is the total amount of taxes paid (including income and payroll taxes and any other additional taxes minus any credits), divided by the taxpayer's total taxable income.

In general, the more brackets and the higher the tax on the top bracket, the greater the progressivity of the system. Federal, state, and local income taxes fall into the progressive tax category. Special sales taxes levied on yachts, jewelry, and other expensive luxuries are also progressive in that they generally fall on people with higher incomes. The Alternative Minimum Tax (AMT) is also a progressive tax originally designed to prevent high income taxpayers from radically reducing or even eliminating their tax bill, although with inflation and other changes to the tax system, it has become less progressive.

Regressive Taxes. These types of taxes do not take into account one's ability to pay, and leave lower-income earners with less disposable after-tax income.

Proportional taxes or *flat taxes* apply the same rate to all incomes. Some recent proposals would replace the multiple-bracketed progressive income tax in the United States with a flat tax, which means a single tax bracket. An example is the Medicare payroll tax, which takes the same proportion of all wage earners' income.

Regressive taxes take a larger percentage of income from low-income groups than from high-income groups. The way the Social Security payroll tax is currently structured is ultimately regressive. It applies the same flat tax rate to all wages or salaries up to the current cap of $90,000. But income above that cap is not taxed at all. Those who earn $90,000 or less, including most women workers, pay taxes on their entire incomes, while those earning double this amount are taxed only on half of their incomes.

When a consumer's after-tax income is considered, sales taxes are also regressive, especially in states or localities that don't exempt groceries and other necessities. In low-income households, predominantly headed by women, virtually all income is spent for daily needs, which means that much of it is subject to sales tax. People who have larger incomes and who do not need to spend all they earn in order to live pay sales taxes on a smaller proportion of their income. The *value-added tax* (VAT), a tax levied in some countries outside the United States on the "value-added" at each step of production and included in the final cost a consumer pays for the product or service, is regressive in the same way.

WHAT HAPPENS WHEN THERE'S NOT ENOUGH TAX REVENUE?

One of the important goals of tax policy is to provide an adequate level of funding for government services. If the amount of money raised through taxes is inadequate, then the government faces a deficit. To pay its bills, it must either cut needed services or borrow money to pay for them. Usually the government does both when it faces a deficit, slashing funding for much-needed activities like education, environmental protection, and health care, and also borrowing money to cover the remaining gap between tax revenues and government spending.

The *deficit* is the amount of money that the government spends over and above what it raises in a given year. In other words, it is the amount of money the government must borrow to meet its budget needs each year. In fiscal year 2004, the U.S. deficit was $413 billion.[8]

The cumulative amount of money that the government owes its lending sources for all borrowed money over the years is called the *national debt*. In November 2004, that debt was just under $7.4 trillion.[45] Like private borrowers, the government must pay interest on its debt, an expense that must be covered each year through the tax revenues for that year. The interest paid on the national debt in 2004 amounted to more than $142.5 billion, or roughly 7 percent of the total budget.[10] Paid by tax dollars, interest payments on the national debt draw on money that might otherwise be used to fund currents needs.

WHAT ELSE DO TAXES DO?

Taxes affect us by reducing the amount of our income we can use for personal spending and by supporting our lives through vital public services. Taxes also affect us in other ways—sometimes by intent, and sometimes through unintended consequences.

For example, since both individuals and businesses respond to financial penalties and rewards, the government sometimes uses taxes to penalize some classes of individuals and some types of behaviors and reward others. These types of taxes tend to be particularly controversial. A classic historical example of a tax used to achieve certain policy goals is the *poll tax*, now illegal, which imposed a tax on each citizen as a precondition to voting. The effect of the poll tax was to prevent those with lower incomes or no wealth, especially African Americans, from exercising their right to vote. Other instances include so-called *sin taxes*, which are meant to discourage tobacco and alcohol use, and *protective tariffs*, designed to discourage the purchase of foreign-made products.

Tax policies also reward certain groups and behaviors through tax deductions and credits. The most familiar tax-rewarded behavior available to an average family is home ownership, with mortgage interest payments deductible from federal income tax. The Child Tax Credit is designed to reduce the financial burden imposed on women, or other primary care-givers of children, who work outside the home. And the Earned Income Tax Credit, a deduction/credit for low-income earners, helps low-income families make ends meet by increasing their after-tax income. Other tax credits invite the middle class to use private rather than public services by subsidizing pri-vate education, health care, and retirement pensions. Tax breaks to individu-als and businesses promote charitable contributions; to corporations they promote the use of energy efficient fuel; and to employers they encourage employee pensions, health insurance, and other fringe benefits.

Tax policy can also have unintended consequences. For example, the so-called marriage penalty, a provision in the tax code that applies to second earners in a married couple who file their tax returns jointly, has been con-sidered a disincentive for married women to work—or for working women to marry. Married women's wages, which in most cases are much lower than their husbands,' have been taxed at higher rates that reflect a couple's joint income, rather than at the lower rate that would apply if women filed as sin-gle taxpayers. While recent changes to the tax code are meant to redress the marriage penalty as it affects some married couples, it still includes unin-tended incentives—and disincentives—for women to marry, work, and have children.[11]

Other consequences of tax policy that have come under increasing scrutiny are the growing gap between rich and poor and the increased ten-dency of U.S. corporations to move operations and jobs offshore.

HAVE TAXES ALWAYS BEEN A WOMAN'S ISSUE?

Women and taxes have a long history. To further their campaign for the vote, suffragists of the eighteenth and early nineteenth centuries took up the Revolutionary-era cry "No taxation without representation!" Because women were denied the vote, suffragists argued, they should not be expected to pay taxes.

In the 1850s, the suffragist Lucy Stone refused to pay taxes on a house that she owned in New Jersey. Susan B. Anthony, at her sentencing for the crime of voting in the 1872 presidential elections, argued, "Your denial of my citizen's right to vote is the denial of my right to consent as one of the governed, the denial of my right of representation as one of the taxed . . . the denial of my sacred rights of life, liberty, [and] property."[12] And in 1907, long-time women's rights activist Susan Pecker Fowler wrote, "As a Tax-Paying Citizen of the United States I am entitled to a voice in Governmental affairs....Having paid this unlawful Tax under written protest for forty years, I am entitled to receive from the Treasury of 'Uncle Sam' the full amount of both Principal and Interest."[13]

While women now have the vote, thanks to the advocacy of these and many other activists, they're still underrepresented in the chambers where tax policy is developed. Women represent more than 50 percent of all taxpayers, but in 2005 women held only 15 percent of Congressional seats and less than 23 percent of the seats in state legislatures.[14] With their distinct status and roles in the paid and unpaid economies, women must continue to demand a say in designing a tax policy that helps foster a fair, equitable, and humane society.

A Personal Story: Taxes and the Social Contract

Stephanie Lindquist talks about her complex relationship to taxes and tax policy: "Taxes were never something I thought too much about, even though I've spent quite a few of my 27 years working in some form or another. Before this year, I relied on my parents to take care of my taxes—and with my meager income, there wasn't much to do.

"This year is different. I work as a tutor with junior high and high school students in math, physics, and Spanish, and my income this past

year—around $18,000—reflects my slow building of clients. In hindsight, I possibly could have put away $50 or $100 a month toward future taxes, but at the time, it didn't seem like an option.

"For one person, $18,000 sounds like a livable income if you really kept to a budget, right? Perhaps in my home state of Minnesota. In San Francisco, rent, food, gas, public transportation, and all those other daily necessities seem to suck away every drop. If I earn on average $1,500 a month, and subtract $680 for rent and utilities (I live with seven people to save money), $230 for groceries, $200 for gas, car maintenance, and public transportation (which I need for my job), $70 for health insurance, $80 for medication, $60 for cell phone (again, for my job), that leaves me with about $50 a week for miscellaneous expenses. I could be in worse shape—I could not have a job, or have a kid, or not have a place to live, so I can't complain. I also have the support of my parents, which allows me to worry just a little bit less. I'm relatively lucky.

"But now that tax season is coming around, I feel anxious every day. What if I don't have enough money to pay the taxes? How do I file? What category of worker do I fall under? If I don't do it right, will I get caught by the IRS? If I take my income statements and receipts to a CPA, will she help me figure out the best way to keep my money in the bank? How much does a CPA cost? What happens if I don't do anything?

"And when I think about where my money will go after it filters its way through the bureaucracy, it makes me angry that I have to pay at all. They don't represent my interests as a queer White young woman. Why should I give money to a government that is using those same funds to do things I despise—like the war in Iraq—and takes money away from programs like education that I feel are necessary for a viable, sustainable society?

"As a citizen of this country, I feel I have a social contract to pay taxes to whatever government is democratically in power. But it's a two-way street. My responsibility, their responsibility. I feel they aren't meeting their responsibility, and I'm not sure yet how I'm going to meet mine."

STRAIGHT TALK ABOUT WOMEN AND TAXES: HOW TO MAKE THE CASE

To those who say: It's your money—the less of it that goes to the government the better.

We say: "Taxes are the price we pay for living in a civilized society." Oliver Wendell Holmes said that in 1904, and the Internal Revenue Service carved it in stone on its main building in Washington, D.C. One hundred years later, much has changed, but not our basic need for services that keep society functioning.

- Nobody wants to give up hard-earned dollars. But nobody wants to give up our schools, our safety, or our economic security either. Taxes pay for our police and firefighters, trains, parks, medical research, national defense, clean food, air, and water and so many other vital goods and services. It's worth the investment, and it makes us stronger as a nation.

- Some people argue that the private sector could provide these services. But do we want private industry to determine how clean our air should be, what level of security is good enough, and whose kids should be able to go to a good school? After all, we can vote for our government, but corporations and private businesses are first and foremost responsible to their owners and stockholders for their bottom line—not to all of us for the quality of our society. Also, a lot of people can't afford the services they need, and some things—like clean air or less congestion on the road-ways—can't be bought by individuals, no matter how many resources they have.

- Another argument says that the government is already taking too much of our money, and if they don't have enough for the services we need, then they can borrow it. But while some borrowing can help a lagging economy, too much deficit spending for current needs means a mounting national debt—and that we're mortgaging our children's futures. While many economists support some level of deficit spending when needed, the level of borrowing today, coupled with enormous tax cuts, will impose a hardship on all of us in the future.

3 | WOMEN AND TAXES: WE *ALL* COULD (AND DO) USE HELP

We need to reframe the discussion of taxes and reveal how taxes are a women's issue. . . . Women's issues are not just about their bodies. They are also about how those bodies survive and thrive in the world, about housing, child-care, nutrition, health services, public safety, education, and basic support for those marginalized by our economic system. Women's issues are basic issues of economic and social justice—and tax policy goes to the heart of those issues.

—Bonnie Thornton Dill, Executive Director, Consortium on Race, Gender, and Ethnicity and Chair, Women's Studies Department, University of Maryland, College Park

Taxes promote a smoothly functioning and humane society by collecting revenues for services and providing tax benefits that encourage certain activities and behavior. Tax revenues support what the public and our elected officials deem necessary and desirable for society's current needs and our future—and they provide a safety net for all of us in times of need.

The government expends its tax resources to meet these needs in two main ways—by directly paying for programs that provide essential services, and by maintaining a complex system of tax deductions, credits, and exemptions that allows individuals and businesses to provide for themselves or their communities. In the following analysis, we use the term "welfare" for both of these systems because they constitute critical forms of government assistance for individuals, families, businesses, and communities, albeit in different forms. Often used as a derogatory term, the word "welfare" has been used to highlight the billions of tax dollars a year that we collectively spend on "corporate welfare" as well as government support to individuals and families in need. But the dictionary reminds us that, far from being a dirty word, "welfare" is the condition of good fortune, health, happiness, prosperity and well-being.

While taxes support a wide range of necessary services—national defense, the criminal justice system, and environmental protections, to name a few—it is in the area of human services that tax and spending policies disproportionately impact women. It is also the area that is often most contentious in debates about these policies. This volume, therefore, focuses on that area of government and the ways in which tax resources serve individuals and families in the United States.

The American public has been encouraged to think that such human services go only to the poor. However, a closer look at the data refutes this perception. The facts are that government tax and spending policies serve middle- and upper-income households and corporations as well as, if not better than they serve low-income families, including the poor. An examination of the two main systems that Washington uses to distribute tax resources to individuals and families—we'll call them the "social welfare" and the "fiscal welfare" systems—shows that the government serves Americans across the economic spectrum.[1]

NOT FOR THE POOR ALONE: THE TWO WELFARE SYSTEMS

The *social welfare* system is highly visible and familiar. Administered by the Social Security Administration, Department of Health and Human Services, and other federal agencies, these tax-funded social welfare programs include both *social insurance programs*, which serve those of all income levels (for example, Social Security and Medicare), and *means-tested programs*, which serve families and individuals whose incomes are so low that they are eligible for public assistance. Together, these programs provide such resources as retirement income, Unemployment Insurance, means-tested cash assistance, food subsidies, housing assistance, and health insurance directly to individuals and families, free of cost or at a cost that is below market value. Given their care-giving responsibilities, large numbers of women in a wide variety of economic situations benefit from these programs, which help support the cost of family life. But due to racial and gender discrimination as well as various family structures, women, especially women of color, and their children often end up proportionately overrepresented in the programs serving only the poor.

The second system—the *fiscal welfare* system—is indirect, largely invisible, and not regarded as welfare. But this system is also meant to provide for the "well-being" of the population. Administered by the Internal Revenue Service (IRS), this system provides enormous benefits to individuals and corporations—indirectly, through tax exemptions, deductions, and credits. Collectively these are defined as "tax expenditures." (Congress adopted the term in 1974, when policymakers began to keep track of the billions of dollars in uncollected taxes lost because of these tax provisions.)[2] Through such tax benefits, the government allows individuals and businesses to lower their tax bills. Due to the misleading perception that these tax expenditures are not government subsidies, few beneficiaries think of themselves as recipients of a tax-supported program. Certainly, they would never call themselves "welfare recipients." The money never leaves a taxpayer's paycheck, never goes to the U.S. Treasury, and in most cases, remains just a mathematical calculation on the tax form. However, given their similar purposes and impact on the U.S. Treasury, the Joint Committee on Taxation equates direct government spending and tax expenditures in discussing the budget.

While the poor and the working class, who are disproportionately women and people of color, are more often served by the social welfare system, middle- and upper-class households receive benefits from both systems far more than those with low incomes. (See table 3.1.)

Taken together, these two systems make it clear that tax-supported benefits are not for the poor alone—and that women, especially women of color and those with low incomes, fare worse in both systems.

TABLE 3.1

THE TWO WELFARE SYSTEMS: NEEDS AND BENEFITS

Need Addressed	Social Welfare System (direct outlays)	Fiscal Welfare System (tax deductions, credits, exemptions)
Basic income support	• Temporary Aid to Needy Families (TANF) • Supplemental Security Income (SSI) • Food Stamps • Unemployment Insurance • Survivors' benefits	• Standard deductions • Deductions for dependents • Child Tax Credit (CTC)* • Earned Income Tax Credit (EITC)*
Health care	• Medicaid • Medicare (including prescription drug benefit)	• Deductions for insurance premiums and medical expenses that exceed 7.5 percent of gross income • Deductions for medical savings accounts • Tax breaks to businesses that provide employee health insurance
Housing	• Rent supplements • Public housing • Shelters for the homeless • Disaster relief funds for housing	• Deductions for mortage interest and state and local property taxes • Lowered capital gains taxes on home sales, and no capital gains taxes on the first $250,000 of value (or $500,000 for a married couple)
Child-care	• Government-subsidized child-care programs, mostly for low-income families	• Credits based on child-care expenses up to $6,000 deduction per-child for single and two-income married couples with children under 13 • Allowance of up to $5,000 in pretax earnings for child-care under employers' "cafeteria plans"

Need Addressed	Social Welfare System (direct outlays)	Fiscal Welfare System (tax deductions, credits, exemptions)
Education	• Free primary and secondary schools • Subsidized public higher education (state university systems) • Educational grants for veterans • Pell Grants • Federal Work-Study • Low-interest student loans	• Exemptions for parents of college students ages 19–23 • Untaxed scholarships • Hope and Lifetime Learning tax credits for postsecondary education
Retirement income	• Social Security retirement benefits	• Tax-free retirement/pension accounts: Individual Retirement Accounts (IRAs), Keogh plans, 401(k)s, Simplified Employee Pensions (SEPs)

* Both the EITC and CTC are technically classified partly as tax outlays and partly as expenditures. The cash refund of each is the outlay component. However, for the purposes of this volume, we are classifying them as expenditures because they are claimed and function as tax credits.

Source: Adapted from Mimi Abramovitz (2001), "Everyone Is Still on Welfare: The Role of Redistribution in Social Policy," *Social Work* 46:4 (July/August), 298.

Basic Income Support for Families. Compared with most other Western industrial nations, the United States has historically provided limited support for families. Instead of direct family allowances like those offered by most European nations, the United States uses the social and fiscal welfare systems to provide limited support for families, underwrite the high cost of raising children, and prepare children for the future.

Forms of basic income support under the social welfare system include both means-tested programs that help those with very low or no incomes, and universal *social insurance programs* for all. The means-tested programs provide support to a variety of individuals, but are especially important to single mothers in helping them cover the cost of raising children. The cash aid provided by *Temporary Aid to Needy Families (TANF)* is supplemented by benefits from the *Food Stamp Program* and programs such as *Women with Infants and Children Supplemental Nutrition Program (WIC)*, which help with the family's food budget. The social welfare system also provides income support through more universal social insurance programs—including *Social Security pensions, Survivors' and Disability benefits*, and *Unemployment Insurance*—that help families and individuals at all income levels with basic support.

The *fiscal welfare system* also helps with basic support, especially home ownership and the cost of raising children, through *standard deductions* or *itemized deductions* for all taxpayers and their dependents. In 2003, for example, the standard deduction, which taxpayers claimed if they were not itemizing their deductions, amounted to $9,500 for married taxpayers filing jointly, and $7,000 for a single head-of-household filer. Those who earned below $209,250 for joint filers or $174,400 for heads-of-household could also exempt $3,050 per child. This structure especially helps low- and moderate-income taxpayers with children, including single parents. In 2003, the income level at which a single tax filer with no children started owing federal income tax was just $9,287 (97 percent of the poverty threshold). A single parent with two children didn't owe federal income taxes until her income exceeded $39,700 (268 percent of the poverty level); and for a married couple with two children, federal income tax liability in 2003 started at $33,328 (179 percent of the poverty level).[3]

Two extremely effective fiscal welfare programs help low- and moderate-income workers support their families: the *Child Tax Credit (CTC)* and the *Earned Income Tax Credit (EITC)*, which reduce the amount of federal tax these workers owe, and also pay a refund to the very lowest-paid workers. The Child Tax Credit, for example, provides two-earner families with annual incomes between $10,500 and $110,000 with a credit of up to $1,000 for each child under the age of seventeen. Since 2001, the CTC has been partially refundable for families whose tax bill is lower than the value of the credit. The EITC is also refundable. What this means is that when a family's income is so low that the credit they are due is a larger amount than the taxes owed, the difference is returned to them in the form of a tax refund. This means that a single mother with two children working full-time at minimum wage and making approximately $13,600 per year (after payroll taxes) is eligible for an EITC of $4,300—that is, she gets a check back for that amount when she files her taxes.[4]

According to Census Bureau data, the EITC lifts 4.9 million people above the poverty level annually, including more than 2.7 million children. In 2002, more than 21 million families and individuals filing federal income tax returns (almost one out of six families who file) took advantage of the EITC.[5]

Some experts would like to see these types of tax credits extended, in particular to account for dependents other than children. "Women are still disproportionately responsible for the long-term care of the elderly, those with disabilities, and the chronically ill," notes Elisabeth Gehl, director of Public Policy at Business and Professional Women/USA. "Yet working women carry that extra burden with little public support. Our society should recognize their contributions and provide tax credits, like those that go to families with young children, to help them balance work and care responsibilities."

Health Care. The United States does not have the kind of publicly financed, universal health care system currently in use in most Western industrialized nations. However, many Americans benefit in some way from tax-funded government programs that support health care.

The social welfare system finances the cost of health care for large numbers of people, many of whom lack employer-based coverage. More than half of those benefiting from these social welfare programs are women. *Medicaid*, the means-tested federal health insurance program for low-income families, serves about 16 million women, 70 percent of the adults covered.[6] Among those served by *Medicare*, the federal program that benefits almost all older Americans (regardless of income), women are 58 percent of recipients over 65 and 85 percent of those 85 and older.[7]

The fiscal welfare system underwrites health care in expanding ways, tending to benefit those who are better-off financially. Firms receive *employer tax breaks* to provide health insurance coverage to their workers, a benefit more likely to reward salaried middle- and upper-income employees than low-income hourly or part-time workers, groups that disproportionately include women. In addition, for those who can afford them, the tax code now contains a variety of *tax-advantaged medical savings accounts*. Self-employed taxpayers can also take *deductions for health insurance premiums*, and taxpayers who itemize can take *deductions for medical costs* if they exceed 7.5 percent of their adjusted gross income. Usually only those with higher incomes can take advantage of these benefits—and since fewer women, especially women of color, have such incomes, they are too often left out.

Housing. The government assists families across the economic spectrum by making the increasingly high cost of housing more affordable.

Through the social welfare system, *public housing*, while less prevalent today than in the past, still serves several million residents—38 percent in families headed by women and just over half headed by people of color.[8] In addition, millions of low-income families receive assistance through *Section 8 Vouchers*, which, although under threat, still provide government subsidies for private rental housing for poor and disabled Americans.

For homeowners—less likely to be women or people of color and more likely to have moderate to higher incomes—the fiscal welfare system offers several subsidies. The largest is the *mortgage interest deduction*, the value of which grows with the size of the mortgage and with a family's income: homeowners in the top fourth of income levels receive 59 percent of these deductions.[9]

Child Care. According to Nancy Folbre, professor of economics at the University of Massachusetts, Amherst, "Parents in general, and mothers in particular, are subsidizing our economic system. They are basically providing the labor on which our economic system depends."[10] In theory, our society recognizes this debt and the importance of raising the next generation of citizens and taxpayers. But in practical, economic terms, the United States provides relatively little publicly supported care for young children, as compared with other Western industrialized countries.

The social welfare system subsidizes both needs-based and universal *child-care and preschool programs*, although considerably more programs are needed to meet the needs of low- and even middle-income working parents, especially single parents, who are usually women. Every day, three out of five preschoolers are in child-care while their mothers and fathers work. The cost of that child-care for those who pay it is high, absorbing a large percentage of low-income families' budgets in particular.

Under the fiscal welfare system, many working- and middle-class women qualify for a special *child-care* or *dependent-care tax credit* based on employment-related care-giving expenses of up to $6,000. Lower-income filers can claim a higher percentage of their care expenses as a credit. While the credit isn't refundable, which limits its value for low-income working parents, it can increase the refund low-income taxpayers get from the EITC.

Education. Taken together, the social and fiscal welfare systems provide an invaluable investment in the nation's children and, therefore, in our collective future.

Through the social welfare system, *public elementary and secondary schools* provide free, tax-supported education to students at all income levels. Almost 90 percent of students in grades one through twelve take advantage of this service.[11] Public high schools serve 92 percent of White, 95 percent of Latino, and 97 percent of African American students.[12] In addition, the social welfare system supports *preschool and after-school programs*, special *programs for children with disabilities*, and *vocational education programs*. Education *vouchers* that cover some of the cost of tuition enable some parents to enroll their children in private schools at public expense. And *publicly funded colleges and universities, Pell Grants*, the *Federal Work-Study program*, and other supports help students meet the high cost of college education.

The fiscal welfare system offers *untaxed scholarships, special learning credits*, and *tax exemptions* for parents of college students ages 19 to 23, all of which help subsidize higher education for many young women and men.

Retirement Income. Both the social welfare and fiscal welfare systems provide retirement income, but within both systems, women tend to receive lower benefits than men. In fact, motherhood, especially single motherhood, is a leading predictor of poverty in old age, because care-giving reduces a woman's overall lifetime earnings and thus her retirement benefits.

Almost all workers and their spouses receive *Social Security retirement benefits* through the social welfare system, but women make up 58 percent of all Social Security beneficiaries age 62 and older, and that number increases steadily as age increases. Women are approximately 70 percent of beneficiaries age 85 and older.[13] A woman's average monthly benefit in 2002 was $714, compared to $1,084 for a man.[14] Women also rely more on Social Security than men do because women's private pensions are fewer and on average less than half of those of men.[15]

One of the most important features of the Social Security retirement system is the progressivity of its benefits—those who earn less over their lifetimes get a higher percentage of their earnings back as retirement benefits than those with higher incomes. This is especially important for women, who tend to earn substantially less over their lifetimes. Moreover, the system does recognize women's care-giving work, at least within the traditional one-earner nuclear family structure, by providing benefits to women as spouses, widows, or divorcees (of marriages of more than ten years), often at higher levels than they would have received based on their own contributions to the system. Unfortunately, single mothers or others who take on responsibility for care-giving outside the traditional marriage structure do not benefit from this provision.

Through the fiscal welfare system, better-off workers with more disposable income can benefit from *tax-deferred programs*: Individual Retirement Accounts (IRAs), 401(k)s, Keogh plans, or Simplified Employee Pensions (SEPs). Because of work patterns and low pay, retired women today are half as likely as men to have private pensions; for those who do, their pensions average half the size of men's. For women over the age of 40 who haven't yet retired, the median 401(k) account balance is $7,000, compared to $20,000 for men.[16]

GOVERNMENT SUPPORT SYSTEMS FAVOR THE "HAVES" OVER THE "HAVE-NOTS"

Both the social welfare system and the fiscal welfare system use tax policy to meet similar needs, and help support families and communities. However, according to Mimi Abramovitz, if we compare spending and benefit levels, and identify the programs most at risk when budgets get cut, it becomes clear that both systems serve the middle- and upper-classes more fully than low-income families, where women and their children tend to predominate.[17]

Benefit Levels. The social welfare system serves all income groups. But nearly universal programs like Unemployment Insurance and Social Security, which serve large numbers of low-, middle-, and upper-income individuals and families, provide significantly more generous and less stigmatized benefits than the means-tested programs just for the poor. Even in the universal programs, people with higher wages and longer work histories receive higher benefits, which means that the affluent tend to do better than those with low incomes. This, in turn, favors men over women. (See table 3.2.) For example, within the Social Security program, even with its progressive benefit formula and its family benefits, retired women and women with disabilities do less well in absolute terms than their male counterparts.

The more affluent also reap a greater share of *fiscal welfare* in various ways.

First, the value of a tax deduction or exemption rises with one's income tax bracket, providing higher savings for those with less need. The value of any deduction for a working family in the lowest bracket would be 10 percent of the deduction, since that is the rate at which the family is taxed, compared to 35 percent for a top-bracket household. And a family with an income so low that they don't owe federal income taxes at all would receive no benefit at all.

Second, many tax benefits are much more likely to be claimed by and have greater value for those who have more money. For example, the mortgage interest payment deduction on home ownership has greater value for those who own more valuable homes and can carry a larger loan with greater interest payments. As a result, the top 10 percent of homeowners receive one-third of all housing tax benefits; the top 25 percent of homeowners get 59 percent of benefits.[18] Census data in 2001 show that the home ownership rate for families headed by women was almost 16 percent lower than the total rate of total home ownership.[19] The home ownership rate for racial and ethnic minorities is also lower than that for Whites: in 2000, only 53 percent of

TABLE 3.2
AVERAGE MONTHLY BENEFITS UNDER PUBLICLY FUNDED PROGRAMS

Program	Average Monthly Benefits (2002)	
Social Insurance Programs		
Unemployment Insurance (individual)	$1,114[i]	
Average Social Security (individual)	$895[ii]	
Retired Worker	$1,084 (men)	$714 (women)
Disabled Worker	$1,028 (men)	$762 (women)
Widow	$751	
Children (survivors under 18)	$395	
Public Assistance Programs		
Supplemental Security Income (individual)	$817[iii]	
Temporary Aid to Needy Families (TANF) (national per capita average)	$143[iv]	

i. U.S. Congress, House, Committee on Ways and Means (2004). *Background Material and Data on Programs within the Jurisdiction of the Committee on Ways and Means* (Green Book), Section 4: Unemployment Compensation, Table 4-1: <http://frwebgate.access.gpo.gov/cgi-bin/useftp.cgi?IPaddress=162.140.64.88&filename= wm006_04.pdf&directory=/disk2/wais/data/108_green_book>.

ii. U.S. Social Security Administration (2003), "Old Age, Survivors and Disability Insurance," *Annual Statistical Supplement*, Table 6.A2: <http://www.ssa.gov/policy/docs/statcomps/supplement/2003/6a.html#table6.a2>.

iii. U.S. Congress, House, Committee on Ways and Means (2004). *Background Material and Data on Programs within the Jurisdiction of the Committee on Ways and Means* (Green Book), Section 3: Supplemental Security Program, Table 3-3: <http://frwebgate.access.gpo.gov/cgibin/useftp.cgi?IPaddress=162.140.64.21&filename=wm 006_03.pdf&directory=/disk2/wais/data/108_green_book>.

iv. U.S. Department of Health and Human Services (2004), *Indicators of Welfare Dependence: Annual Report to Congress*, Appendix A: Program Data: Aid to Families with Dependent Children (AFDC) and Temporary Assistance for Needy Families (TANF): <http://aspe.hhs.gov/hsp/indicators04/>.

Source: Adapted from Mimi Abramovitz (2001), "Everyone Is Still on Welfare: The Role of Redistribution in Social Policy," Social Work 46:4 (July/August), 300.

Asians and 46 percent of African Americans and Hispanics owned homes, compared to about 72 percent of non-Hispanic Whites.[20]

Third, tax benefits provided by the fiscal welfare system are not limited to support for basic necessities, as are most social welfare services. Tax deductions are available for mortgage interest payments on beach vacation homes or as incentives to pursue tax-free investments. Capital gains are taxed at lower rates than wages, and deductions for charitable giving are only available to those who itemize their deductions on their tax returns, almost always higher-income taxpayers rather than low-income earners.

Fourth, tax-favored retirement benefits, medical savings accounts, and education vouchers encourage taxpayers to use and support private rather than public sector programs. Since better-off families are more likely to be able to afford such choices, low-income households are left to rely on increasingly underfunded public sector services, like public health services and schools. Even important programs like the EITC and CTC that provide significant benefits for those with low and moderate incomes do not fully compensate those families for the loss of public services. When services like child-care or Medicaid are cut, such families are often not able to afford their replacement in the private sector, even with the tax credits.

Fifth and finally, many low-income families may not even know they are eligible for tax benefits or understand how to claim the credits they are due. For example, as valuable as it is, the EITC fails to benefit many eligible families because they fail to claim it. According to the Children's Defense Fund, about 3 million eligible families with children—about 15 percent of the total eligible families—did not know to file for the credit. Similarly, nearly 25 percent of low-income taxpayers with children did not claim the newly refundable Child Tax Credit in 2001, collectively losing $238 million.[21] Organizations like the National Women's Law Center and even local governments like New York City have undertaken publicity campaigns to make low-income families aware of these credits.

This discrepancy in benefit levels is even greater when race is considered. Occupational segregation by race, differential rates of unemployment for people of color, and various forms of racism continue to influence job, educational, and housing opportunities. This means that access to social and fiscal welfare is not equitable across racial groups. Political scientist Linda Faye Williams has examined key social and fiscal welfare programs, concluding that Whites and African Americans differ substantially in the benefits they get from both systems.[22] Working closely with analysts from the U.S. Census Bureau, Williams used data from the Current Population Survey (CPS) and from the Survey of Income and Program Participation (SIPP) to examine racial differences both in access to key social and fiscal welfare programs and in levels of benefits received. Because such data is hard to come by and rarely analyzed, her results are striking. She found significant inequities in access to both important social insurance programs and to fiscal welfare (what she calls "hidden welfare").

Using data for 2001, Williams found that while African Americans were overrepresented relative to their share of the population in receiving benefits from means-tested programs, they are underrepresented in many of the most valuable social insurance programs—Medicare, Social Security, and Social Security survivor payments. Given their overall representation in the population, African Americans are only 88 percent as likely as Whites to receive Social Security and 81 percent as likely to receive Medicare.[23] African Americans were even more underrepresented in key fiscal welfare programs, including private health insurance, private pension plans, and tax deductions for mortgage interest payments. They were about half as likely in relation to their share of the population to get private pensions, and even less likely to be able to claim the mortgage interest deduction.[24]

Williams found significant and even more troubling differences between African Americans and Whites in a variety of other programs. Specifically, African American's average annual benefits or income from Veterans' payments were $919 lower than those received by Whites; their Workers Compensation benefits were $470 lower per year; their Social Security retirement and survivor payments were $1,416 and $4,019 lower per year, respectively; and their disability payments were $1,739 lower per year.[25]

The race-based disparities in fiscal welfare benefits were also high. Examining tax credits or deductions for mortgage interest, pension plans, or government education assistance, Williams found that the tax benefits received by African Americans were significantly lower than those received by Whites: $1,918 lower for the benefit from private pensions, $1,279 less annually in educational tax benefits, and a whopping $3,156 lower for the mortgage interest tax deduction.[26] Moreover, in an explanation of her methodology, Williams noted that because the Census includes Latinos in both the White and Black categories, the actual benefit amounts for non-Latino Whites are probably even higher, meaning that the racial disparities would also be considerably greater.

Williams concludes that these racial disparities are a result of both market forces—specifically, discrimination in the labor force—*and* tax and social policies—specifically, the multitude of policies that provide different benefits to Whites and people of color, to men and women, and to those with greater or lesser economic resources.

A 2005 report from the Tax Policy Center and the Urban Institute echoes Williams's findings, revealing differences in benefit levels from the Child Tax Credit. According to the report, in 2002, almost 50 percent of African American children and 46 percent of Hispanic children did not receive a full credit because their families' earnings were too low. Only 18 percent of White families had incomes too low for the full credit. The result: an African American child received on average $564 from the credit; an Hispanic child, $638; and a White child, $721.[27]

Spending Levels. The social welfare system serves all income levels, but the overwhelming majority of dollars go to programs serving households that are better-off financially. In 2003, the federal government spent $1,322 billion (or 61 percent of total federal outlays)[28] on programs that serve large numbers of people but do not consider need as a criterion for receiving aid—including Unemployment Insurance and Social Security for retirees, survivors, and disabled workers. In contrast, only $274 billion (or 12 percent of total federal outlays)[29] went for Medicaid, Temporary Aid for Needy Families (TANF), and other means-tested public assistance programs that serve families in greater need.[30] These means-tested social welfare programs also have far more restrictive eligibility rules than programs open to the middle- and upper-classes.

"Spending" for the fiscal welfare system refers to taxes not collected—that is, revenues lost to tax credits, deductions, and exemptions. These tax expenditures cost the government considerably more than the amounts spent in most social welfare categories. In 2002, $609 billion was spent on fiscal welfare. This is $320 billion more than was spent on non-defense discretionary programs (like education), $323 billion more than on means-tested programs (like Medicaid), and $156.9 billion more than on Social Security. This funding differential plays out in concrete ways: tax expenditures for housing amounted to $57.2 billion in 2003, costing the U.S. Treasury almost twice as much as direct federal expenditures for rental housing subsidies and public housing programs for lowest-income households.[31]

Vulnerability to Budget Cuts. Highly visible and subject to regular budget review, most social welfare programs, especially the means-tested programs that serve low-income women, are more vulnerable to Congressional budget cuts than fiscal welfare programs. For example, in its 2006 budget proposal, the administration of George W. Bush called for significant reductions in a number of key programs for low- and middle-income Americans—despite the fact that in 2004 the number of Americans living in poverty went up for the fourth year in a row.[32] Specifically, over the next ten years the administration would like to spend $45 billion less for Medicaid (although the number of uninsured is rising), $1.1 billion less on Food Stamps (300,000 fewer people served), and $18 billion less on all domestic discretionary programs—programs such as education, environmental protection, and other programs not related to the Department of Defense, international affairs, or homeland security.

According to researchers from the Center on Budget and Policy Priorities, while programs serving low-income families account for about 20 percent of all government expenditures, they may well constitute almost half of the budget cuts in 2006 because other costly and more politically popular programs are likely to be taken "off the table" for significant cuts.[33] However, in recent years, those who want to shrink governmental programs have even targeted universal social welfare programs like Social Security and Medicare, which had been relatively protected by their popularity among middle- and upper-income groups (who are most likely to vote).

Less visible and less stigmatized, the fiscal welfare system is less subject to the perils of the budget process. Tax credits, deductions, and exemptions attract comparatively little public attention and far less Congressional over-sight than what normally accompanies direct spending. They require neither annual Congressional appropriation nor reauthorization, except if and when scheduled to expire. Because they tend to have powerful interests backing them and because they create little if any new governmental bureaucracy, these tax benefits win Congressional approval more easily and remain on the books longer than direct spending programs. In fact, even as deep cuts in dis-cretionary programs are implemented for programs that support low-income and poor households, the Bush administration is also proposing to phase out two tax provisions put in place with the 1990 deficit-reduction package—enacted under the first President Bush—to limit deductions and exemptions for high-income households. Ninety-seven percent of those ben-efiting would be people with incomes over $200,000.[34]

In brief, the "welfare system" for people at the top not only pays more but is more permanent and relatively more secure. The discrepancy between the two systems has grown larger during the last two decades as many social pro-grams, as well as the concept of direct government service, have come under intense attack.

HOW DO THE TWO SYSTEMS AFFECT WOMEN?

Women are the majority of recipients of the social welfare system's social insurance and means-tested public assistance programs. Women of all income levels benefit greatly from the wide range of services the system offers. In contrast, women, especially women of color, are underrepresented among those who receive the benefits provided by the fiscal welfare system—benefits like mortgage interest deductions and deductions for pri-vate retirement accounts or health care. Within both the social and the fiscal welfare systems, higher-earning taxpayers receive greater benefits—and women, who earn less and spend more years out of the labor force than men, lose out.

Moreover, the discrepancies between social welfare and fiscal welfare have widened during the past two decades. Changes sold as tax "reforms" have expanded the fiscal welfare system, while social welfare "reforms" have translated into cuts in benefits and services especially important to women. As the national debates about tax reform and government spending intensify, the role of fiscal welfare and the importance of the social welfare system must be part of the debate. Women's voices and experiences must figure centrally in these discussions.

A Personal Story: The Dual Welfare System— A Special Case

For the past 25 years, Guadalupe Quinn has been a community activist working on social justice issues, especially immigrant rights. As a Latina—her family came to the United States from Mexico when she was three years old—she knows firsthand the challenges that face immigrants, including tax issues.

Quinn remembers the overflowing shoebox her father used to keep the receipts he took to the person who prepared his taxes. She also has vivid memories of accompanying him to translate at tax time when she was in grade school. Later her father found a Spanish-speaking tax pre-parer, so she didn't have to do that anymore. But language remains a problem for many immigrant families when tax time rolls around. In Quinn's home community, a local Latino community organization helps immigrant families with tax questions and advice. But not all immigrants can count on this kind of help.

Quinn, who works half-time as an organizer with a statewide immigrant rights organization in Oregon, and her husband, who has retired from his school system job, don't get many tax breaks these days. Their son is grown and there is not much they can write off. But she rec-ognizes that she is better off that most of the families she works with. "Many of the families we work with—they are just getting by. Their income is limited. They get what little they get from work, and they take care of their kids. Taxes are overwhelming and it is all they can do to be sure they get their taxes filed right, something that makes them very nervous. And they sure aren't getting a lot of tax breaks."

Undocumented immigrants face another set of problems. Of course, like other workers, most have withholding tax and Social Security deducted from their paychecks. In order to get any of this money back, they have to file a tax return, but undocumented workers don't have Social Security numbers. Quinn notes that undocumented workers are encouraged to get an Individual Taxpayer Identification Number (ITIN), which allows them to file tax returns. "Its good that having a taxpayer ID number enables folks to file their taxes," says Quinn, "but a lot of people are afraid to get that ID number because they are afraid the government will come after them. Even though the IRS says it doesn't share information with other government agencies, it's hard, especially these days, for most immigrants to believe that. And if a family doesn't file a tax return they don't get back any of their withholding, even though most have incomes low enough that they would otherwise be eligible to get money back. And unless they become naturalized, they can't ever collect Social Security. So they pay in, but they don't get back what other workers do." Another twist: undocumented workers who do file their taxes with the ITIN are not eligible to get the Earned Income Tax Credit. Congress specifically excludes them from being able to take advantage of the most significant tax break available to low-income families.

Nor do undocumented workers have any say in how their money is spent, because while they pay taxes, they cannot vote. But even having a vote doesn't mean taxpayers such as Quinn feel well represented in the decisions policymakers have made about taxes and government spending. Guadalupe Quinn is deeply concerned about how little control she—and indeed, most of us—has over how the money is spent. She thinks today's federal spending priorities are far from those that would really help women, communities of color, or working people generally. "My concern is that we—most of us—don't have a real voice in where that money goes. We all know we pay taxes for general things like schools and roads and other things we all need. But most of it goes to defense, the military, not to constructive things that really enhance people's lives." And for someone who works every day to promote social

*justice, to help people have a say about the issues that affect their every-
day lives, that disconnect is close to the top of the list of things she wants
to see changed.*

STRAIGHT TALK ABOUT WOMEN AND TAXES: HOW TO MAKE THE CASE

To those who say: Poor people get a free ride thanks to my taxes!

We say: We all receive assistance from the government—be it social insurance
or means-tested benefits through the social welfare system, or tax benefits
and deductions through the fiscal welfare system. Just because we don't call
the tax-related benefits "welfare" doesn't meant that they aren't effectively
providing generous subsidies. In fact, those with more tend to get more.

As a society, we're in this together—and most of us do feel an obligation
to the very young and very old, those with disabilities, the mentally ill, and
those who are most vulnerable in our society. Why?

- It's the only way to build the kind of society that most of us want to live
  in, a society that provides everyone an opportunity to succeed and a solid
  safety net in times of need—making it possible for most people to be productive and economically secure. After all, we're all better off when our
  neighbors are doing well too.
- It's the smart thing to do because it helps ensure our economic stability
  and competitiveness. We can't afford to consign a large proportion of our
  population to the dust heap.
- It's the right thing to do. Leaving those most vulnerable to the mercy of
  whatever might befall them is not socially responsible.
- If you think you don't personally benefit from government welfare, think
  again! Tax deductions, exemptions, and credits—what we've called "fiscal
  welfare" programs—provide even more support to the middle class, the
  wealthy, and private businesses. Mortgage deductions, child-care credits,
  small business write-offs, investment credits, deductions for charitable
  contributions and medical savings accounts, and other tax "benefits"

mean that middle-class and wealthy people rely on government programs along with everyone else.

- We may not think of these fiscal welfare programs as government subsidies. But, they are—Congress labels these benefits "tax expenditures" because they cover the same needs as social spending and translate into the loss of billions of dollars in uncollected taxes.[35] But whatever we call them, it is clear that tax-supported benefits are not for the poor alone.

4 | HOW WE GOT HERE: A BRIEF HISTORY OF U.S. TAX POLICY

I know firsthand how a vigorous and effective government can intercede in the economy in order to address the country's needs. I grew up during the Great Depression, and I earned a Ph.D. in economics at a time when a progressive theory of economics was driving public policy. Those policies provided the desperately needed means to expand government action and bring the United States out of the Depression and into an era of unprecedented economic growth for almost all Americans. Now, more than 40 years later, I am deeply worried about the direction that prevailing economic policies are taking us, policies that extol the virtues of small government, low taxes, and unrestrained privatization.

—Mariam Chamberlain, Founding President and Resident Scholar, The National Council for Research on Women

The structure of our tax system—how progressive or regressive it is, what types of income are taxed, and the rates of taxation—determines who pays how much of the nation's bills and how much money is available for government services. How did our complex system of taxes, tax benefits, and tax expenditures develop?

The overall tax system has become less progressive over time, but especially since the mid-1970s. At that time, forces opposed to "big government" used changes in the U.S. and global economies to justify attacks on policies that had been put in place during the New Deal of the 1930s and the Great Society of the 1960s—policies designed to promote economic growth, political stability, and the economic security of U.S. families. Pressed by business interests and armed with conservative economic theories, federal, state, and local governments began to change tax law. They altered the way they taxed income from work, wealth, and corporate profits, and increased the use of tax credits, deductions, and exemptions. States and localities increased their reliance on regressive taxes, especially the sales tax. All of this combined to make the U.S. tax system less progressive and, along with changes in spending priorities, reduced the revenues available to fund the public programs that had been so helpful to women and their families.

Not surprisingly, during the 1980s and 1990s, middle-class and low-income families began to feel squeezed by these changes. Many living-wage jobs were disappearing, and wages began to stagnate even as a two-decade-long pattern emerged of unprecedented growth in the pretax income of the richest Americans. The mounting income inequality and changes in the tax philosophy—capped by dramatic tax cuts in 2001 and 2003—have fallen heavily on women, who represent a growing number of taxpayers[1] and who, with their families, often rely on government services.

A brief tour through the history of our tax system shows how it has changed since taxes were first levied and how those changes have affected women.

THE FIRST FEDERAL TAXES

Congress first used its constitutional right to levy federal taxes in 1789, imposing a tariff that became the chief source of federal revenues until the outbreak of the Civil War in 1861. From shortly after the Civil War until 1913, almost 90 percent of federal revenues were still collected from excise taxes.[2] In 1913, the Sixteenth Amendment of the Constitution gave the Congress the power to tax wages (individual income tax) and wealth (gift and estate taxes, for example). Since almost 90 percent of federal revenues were collected from excise taxes on luxury items and since the government taxed income from wealth more heavily than income from work, the elite shouldered nearly all of the tax bill. As a result, less than 1 percent of the population paid federal income taxes.[3] Promoted as a tax on "surplus" incomes, the "class tax," or a tax on those with higher incomes, was the main source of federal revenues.

THE INCOME TAX: FROM A CLASS TAX TO A MASS TAX

In 1945, to pay for World War II, the federal government converted the class tax into a mass tax. It raised the income tax rate for those in the top bracket (income over $400,000) to a record 94 percent, and extended the federal income tax downward to more and more wage earners. The number of returns grew from 15 million in 1940 to 50 million in 1945, affecting almost three-quarters of the population, including many women. As a consequence, federal revenues also soared from $7 billion to $50 billion.[4] Although Congress lowered the top tax rate to 91 percent following World War II, the basic structure of the tax—25 tax brackets, high tax rates for high incomes, and exemptions for low earners—meant that people's tax rates were tailored to their income level.[5] This worked to the advantage of women as low earners and low wealth holders.

During the 1950s, the Korean conflict soaked up tax revenues, but Congress had enough money, with mild deficit spending, to expand the range of public services that had proved so useful to individual Americans since the New Deal. Government programs increased access to affordable education (the G.I. Bill), home ownership (Federal Housing Administration and Veteran's Administration mortgages), decent jobs (massive public works projects),[6] a national highway system, and employment and training programs. By the early 1970s, Congress had added job development (Manpower Development, Comprehensive Employment and Training Act [CETA]), health care (Medicaid for the poor and Medicare for all older Americans), Food Stamps, the Earned Income Tax Credit, and a host of other services, including programs for health and mental health, education, and employment that supported families and helped support women's care-giving work in the home. For all the grumbling, in 1972, people told pollsters they considered the federal income tax the "fairest" of all taxes.[7]

Beginning in the mid-1970s, however, changes in tax policy gradually undermined the basic progressivity of the tax code and led to a sharp fall-off in public support for federal tax law. Washington dropped the rate for the top earners (those with incomes over $200,000) from 91 percent in the years from 1950 to 1963 to a low of 71 percent in the 1970s. Pressed by business lobbies and Political Action Committees, Congress enacted the Nixon administration's "business incentive" initiatives and began to view tax breaks for business and wealthy individuals as the solution to every social and economic problem that emerged. Meanwhile, Congress raised the tax rates on the middle class and let inflation erode the value of their exemptions. By the end of the 1970s, the public was becoming increasingly dissatisfied with the federal tax system. The same polls that had found widespread public approval for the income tax in 1972 now found the opposite. By the early 1980s, more and more people each year were citing the federal income tax as the "least fair" tax.[8]

THE REAGAN REVOLUTION: SUPPLY-SIDE ECONOMICS

The trend toward a less progressive tax code accelerated in the 1980s, with the election of President Ronald Reagan. A shift in tax philosophy and attacks on "big government" accompanied his election and were instrumental in further eroding the progressivity of the tax system. "Trickle-down" or "supply-side" economics posited that economic growth required more savings and investment by wealthy individuals and large corporations, and fewer "excessive" claims on the government by those in need. Also known as "Reaganomics," this approach justified collecting a smaller proportion of tax revenue from the very wealthy and reducing the role of government in providing basic services to individuals and families. Economist, author, and commentator Julianne Malveaux has noted that the rhetoric of Reaganomics succeeded in transforming not only the tax system itself, but also the public's perception of it. As Malveaux writes, "The Reagan Revolution worked. . . . [H]e set up the dialogue about reducing taxation and shrinking the size of government. After Reagan, we began to hear in the popular discourse that government is bad—too much government is bad."[9]

While changes in the economy and in the political balance in Washington caused temporary interruptions, accelerations, and reversals in the process, Congress over the next two and a half decades gradually implemented the shift in policy by reducing the number of tax brackets, lowering the tax rates on high income, and increasing tax expenditures like deductions, exemptions, and credits. These changes have far-reaching implications for Americans at all economic levels.

Fewer Tax Brackets. The 25 brackets in place at the end of World War II held steady through most of the 1970s, which meant that the tax system could make relatively fine distinctions between those who earned more and those who earned less, and tax them at different rates. Congress reduced the number of brackets to 15 in 1982 and then to three in 1991, before inching the number back up to six in 2004. With fewer brackets, the new tax code applies a specific tax rate to a much larger range of incomes within the bracket. Those at the top pay less than they did under the more differentiated system that had placed them in a higher tax bracket and applied higher rates. Recent proposals to "simplify" the tax system by reducing or eliminating the brackets altogether would mean that an even smaller proportion of the tax bill would be paid by those at the top of the income scale.

Lower Tax Rates. Since the Reagan years, the government has also lowered tax rates. The rate for the top earners, which fell from 91 percent in the post–World War II era to 71 percent in the 1970s, began to plummet. The supply-siders cut the top rate to 50 percent in 1982, and then to 28 percent in 1988, its lowest level since 1920. While rising deficits—under Presidents Ronald Reagan, George H. W. Bush, and Bill Clinton—drove the rates up again, in the last several years even the ballooning deficit has not halted the drop in tax rates. In 2003, despite record-level deficits, the top tax rate dropped again to 35 percent under the administration of George W. Bush.[10] Overall, the effective tax rate for the richest 1 percent of households dropped 57 percent between 1948 and 1999, while that of median-income Americans almost quadrupled.[11] The rate for top earners dropped another 20 percent between 2001 and 2004, from a rate of 33.0 percent to 26.7 percent.[12]

Increased Tax Expenditures. The progressivity of the tax system also lost ground over the years as the introduction of tax credits, deductions, and exemptions reduced the tax bill for corporations and individuals earning enough to itemize deductions. In 1993 there were 110 more tax expenditures than there had been when the corporate and individual income taxes were established in 1909 and 1913, respectively.[13] The number continued to rise in the following decade: in 2004 there were 146 corporate and individual tax expenditures available. In fact, it has been estimated that the amount of taxes *not* collected between 1996 and 2002 due to these tax expenditures would have more than paid off the entire national debt, which in 2002 stood at $3.4 trillion.[14] Looking forward, the Joint Committee on Taxation has estimated that the five largest expenditures alone will reduce tax revenues by $2.1 trillion for fiscal years 2005 through 2009.[15]

In brief, over the last sixty years, as record numbers of women entered the labor force and joined the ranks of income taxpayers, the structure of the federal income tax was becoming increasingly less progressive.

FROM TAXING WEALTH TO TAXING WORK

The government taxes both work income and investment income. But since the Reagan years, it has undermined the progressivity of the U.S. tax code by increasing the proportion of taxes on income from employment and reducing taxes on income from wealth. In fact, columnist Allan Sloan predicted in 2004 that, as changes in tax policy take root "the income tax will become a misnomer—it will really be a salary tax. Almost all income taxes would come from paychecks—80 percent of the income for most families, less than half for the top one percent. Meanwhile taxpayers receiving dividends, interest and capital gains, known collectively as investment income, would have a much lighter burden than salary earners—or maybe none at all."[16]

While annual income governs a family's day-to-day economic comfort level, wealth is the foundation for a family's long-term security.[17] Wealth includes financial assets like bank accounts and pension savings plus the value of property, investments, and unincorporated businesses.[18] While wealth varies widely by gender and race, for many families, the main source of wealth is equity in their own home and possibly a pension for retirement. These resources represent a "nest egg" rather than a substantial source of ongoing income. For the affluent, on the other hand, wealth can represent a substantial source of income in the form of interest, dividends, or gains from the sale of investments.

Congress first taxed income from wealth—capital gains, dividend income, and large inherited estates—during the period of social reform known as the Progressive Era (1896–1917). In proposing the federal estate tax in 1906, President Theodore Roosevelt explained, "The man of great wealth owes a particular obligation to the State because he derives special advantages from the mere existence of government."[19] During the Great Depression of the 1930s, Congress increased taxes on wealth under the leadership of Franklin D. Roosevelt, who declared, "Great accumulations of wealth cannot be justified on the basis of personal and family security. . . . Such inherited economic power is as inconsistent with the ideals of this generation as inherited political power was inconsistent with the ideals of the generation which established our government."[20]

The rates for estate taxes held steady from the 1930s until the late 1970s. Then, in the early 1980s, with the growing influence of the supply-siders, Congress began to cut taxes on wealth and income from wealth. These changes have continued over subsequent decades, dramatically undermining the progressivity of the U.S. tax code.

Capital Gains. Introduced in 1913, capital gains taxes apply to profits made on the sale of stocks, real estate, and other financial assets. The rate has varied over the years, reaching 39 percent in the mid-1930s, dropping to 25 percent until the mid-1960s, and rising again in the mid-1970s to 39 percent. In 1998, Congress slashed the capital gains rate to 20 percent and then down to 15 percent by 2003. This change had the greatest benefit for the most wealthy, who derive more than half of their income from the sale of assets.[21]

Dividend Income. In 1936, Congress started to tax dividends paid to investors in corporate stocks and bonds. Until 2003, Congress taxed them as ordinary income, with the tax rate varying according to the taxpayer's income tax bracket. This meant that the top marginal dividend rates fell from a high of 70 percent in the 1970s, to 50 percent in 1982, to 28 percent in 1988, and then rose again to 39.6 percent in 1993.[22] In 2003, Congress stopped taxing dividends as ordinary income, instead setting a flat rate of 15 percent—the same as for capital gains—for most taxpayers receiving dividend income. (Those relatively few low-income taxpayers with dividend income pay 5 percent.) This means that the top rate on dividends for most taxpayers dropped by 79 percent in about 30 years.[23] These tax cuts greatly benefit the top 0.2 percent of tax filers—those with incomes over $1 million—who collect 20 percent of all dividend earnings.[24] But they offer no savings to the 83 percent of households that receive no dividend income.[25] In fact, because of the 2003 cut, the top 0.2 percent of tax filers saved an average of $27,000 a year in taxes, compared with just $29 for those earning between $30,000 and $40,000.[26]

Estates. Introduced in 1916, the estate tax, or inheritance tax, is levied on assets above a certain value that are passed on to heirs when an individual dies. Marginal rates rise gradually according to the size of the estate. Originally 10 percent on estates over $5 million, the top marginal estate tax rate grew to 70 percent on fortunes greater than $50 million by 1935, with the tax providing 11 percent of federal revenue.[27] The estate tax stayed in this range until the 2001 tax cuts, which gradually cut the top marginal rate to 45 percent, and raised the amount of wealth exempted from any estate tax to $3.5 million, effective in 2009.[28] The 2001 law, if left unchanged, would repeal the estate tax altogether for one year in 2010, after which the law would "sunset," or expire, and the estate tax would return to pre-2001 levels.[29] But in April 2005, the House of Representatives voted to make the 2001 law permanent, and to repeal the estate tax altogether. The Joint Committee on Taxation has estimated that such a change in the law would cost the U.S. Treasury $290 billion between 2006 and 2015.[30]

Although the Senate rejected the House bill in mid-2005, the issue remains alive, and the rhetoric surrounding the estate tax debate continues to be especially heated. Anti–estate tax lobbyists have tried to portray the estate tax as a "death" tax, falling on whatever assets any of us hold at the time of our death. Jennifer Roback Morse of the Independent Women's Forum said, "The heirs of many farmers, ranchers and small business owners must liquidate their business just to pay estate taxes."[31] But when challenged, the pro-repeal American Farm Foundation could not cite a single example of a farm lost to the estate tax. Nor could Neil Harl, an Iowa State University economist whom Midwest farmers turn to for tax advice, find such a case. Currently family businesses and farms account for less than 3 percent of the assets in taxable estates valued at less than $5 million.[32]

In fact, in 2001, only two percent of estates were taxed federally.[33] Right now, about half of all the wealth in the United States is inherited, but the federal government levies a tax only on inheritances of over $1.5 million, with only 1 out of every 15,587 people in the United States, including those who own family businesses and farms, paying an estate tax. Recent polls have shown that Americans who are well informed about the estate tax favor estate tax reform over an estate tax repeal by a margin of 67 to 27 percent.[34]

THE DISAPPEARING CORPORATE INCOME TAX

Since 1909, the Internal Revenue Service has taxed corporate as well as individual income. The progressivity of this type of tax has also declined over the years. Between 1962 and 2000, Congress cut the top corporate tax rate from 52 percent to 35 percent.[35] According to the Organization for Economic Cooperation and Development, the United States now ranks 22nd of 29 industrial nations in corporate tax revenues as a percentage of the Gross Domestic Product (GDP).[36] In 2000, an estimated 94 percent of U.S. corporations and 89 percent of foreign corporations doing business in the United States paid less than 5 percent of their total incomes in taxes.[37] In 2002 and 2003, corporate tax receipts measured against the GDP fell to 1.2 percent—the lowest level since the 1930s, with the exception of one year early in the Reagan administration.[38] In 2004, corporate taxes rose slightly to 1.6 percent of the GDP; they are projected to fall to 1.5 percent in 2011 and thereafter.[39] Although there was a jump in corporate tax revenues of about $50 billion between 2004 and 2005, this increase resulted from the expiration of one large business tax cut made two years earlier. By 2007, corporate tax rates are expected to stabilize after an initial increase in 2005 and 2006.[40]

The effects of these changes in corporate taxation go beyond the decreased revenues from this sector. In addition, by *not* taxing profits made abroad, tax policy has also encouraged U.S.-owned multinational corporations and others to export production.[41] As a *New York Times* editorial on 17 September 2004 noted, "Some offshore entities are merely tax-reducing way stations. In other places, American companies have legitimate business operations, which are often coupled with aggressive tax-avoidance strategies." Whichever is the case, the flight of business to countries where wages and

GRAPH 4.1
U.S. CORPORATE INCOME TAXES AS SHARE OF GDP

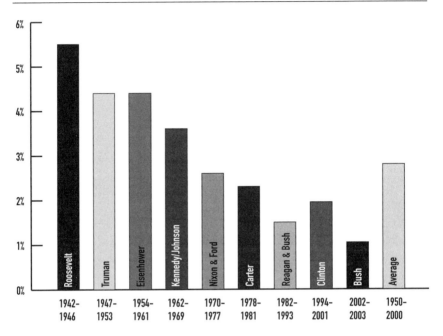

Source: Citizens for Tax Justice (2003), *More Corporate Tax Shelters on the Way?*: <http://www.ctj.org/pdf/corp1003.pdf>.

taxes are lower highlights the pressing need for innovative strategies to encourage corporations to keep production in the United States, and require them to contribute a reasonable amount to society no matter where their production takes place.

THE GROWING BILL FOR PAYROLL TAXES

Social Security is a landmark entitlement program that has almost single-handedly reduced poverty among the elderly, especially older women, and provided important economic security for retirees and their families, the disabled, and many children of deceased workers. Its progressive benefit formula helps reduce poverty because low-income workers receive a higher proportion of their tax payments back in benefits than higher-income work-ers, who pay more into the system. With its inflation-protected benefits, its progressive formula for determining benefits, and its recognition of non-wage-earning spouses and survivors, it is a particularly important program for women, who tend to live longer, yet have lower lifetime earnings. In fact, women constitute about 57 percent of all adult Social Security beneficiaries and receive about 50 percent of the total benefits paid (including survivor and disability payments).[42]

In contrast, the payroll tax that funds the program is not progressive. All workers pay the same rate on their income up to $90,000. But workers earn-ing more than $90,000 do not pay any Social Security taxes on income over that amount, so they effectively contribute a smaller share of their earnings to the system than someone earning $90,000 or less. Since a higher propor-tion of women than men earn under $90,000 women lose out as lower-paid workers because of the regressivity of the tax structure.

Because the Social Security tax rate has increased dramatically, and because the revenue it brings in represents a greater share of overall U.S. tax revenue, it has contributed in a significant way to the declining progressivity of the overall tax system. Since the mid-1970s, Congress has raised the Social Security tax rate and the amount of income subject to it. At the same time, Congress lowered taxes on income, wealth, and corporations. In fact, the income cap for Social Security has risen steadily, from $4,800 in 1960 to $90,000 in 2005, while the tax rate has risen from 6.5 percent in 1960 to 10.6 percent in the 1980s to 12.4 percent in 2005.[43]

As a result of these trends, the Social Security tax during the last 40 years has consumed a growing proportion of wages, although the expansion of the Earned Income Tax Credit (EITC) has to some extent offset this increase for mid- and low-income families. While employers pay half of employees' Social Security tax (currently 6.2 percent), most economists acknowledge that these payments effectively come out of what would otherwise be paid to workers. According to the latest data, more than 75 percent of workers earn-ing under $100,000 pay more in payroll taxes, including their own and the employer's share, than they do in federal income taxes.[44] For example, a single mother with one child earning $23,000 a year has a combined employee and employer Social Security tax liability of $3,519. Although she could receive a $1,000 CTC and $1,208 from the EITC, the Social Security tax still represents a significant deduction from her paycheck. And recent tax cuts—focused primarily on reducing income, dividend, and estate taxes—have provided no relief for those at the bottom of the income scale. Even when their income tax bills seem reasonable in terms of their total incomes, payroll taxes continue to take a big bite out of their salaries. And they are still paying a higher proportion of their salaries to payroll taxes than those who earn more than $90,000.

High levels of payroll taxes take on a special significance in an age of high federal budget deficits. As increasing federal expenditures combine with tax cuts to enlarge the deficit, the federal government borrows from other sources to pay for its daily operations. One of these sources is the Social Security Trust Fund—the money that has been raised through Social Security payroll taxes and is meant to be held in reserve to pay for Social Security benefits in the future. While the Trust Fund has been enriched by increases in Social Security taxes over and above what is needed for current Social Security expenses, any surplus is meant to provide adequate funding when the baby boomers retire. But instead, the Trust Fund is now being used to pay for current government expenditures. This means we're drawing on revenues raised through payroll taxes, which excludes incomes over $90,000, in order to make up for revenues not raised through more progressive taxes like the income tax. Essentially, then, we are asking less wealthy Americans to pay an even larger share of current expenses—and we're going to ask future taxpayers to pay it back, with interest!

While many critics assert that changes are needed to ensure the long-term solvency of the Social Security system, other experts assure us that thanks to increases in the tax over the past twenty years, the Social Security system is in better financial health than it has been for most of its history,[45] and is solvent until at least 2041. If tax levels remain unchanged, the system will still be able to pay 68 percent of full benefits through 2079.[46]

In fact, some of the proposals from Social Security's critics—for example, privatizing the program by replacing the current system with individual retirement accounts—do not in any way address issues of long-term financial viability. For many low- and middle-income earners, such changes would undermine, rather than enhance, their future financial security. These proposals also fail to address the basic regressiveness of the tax that supports the program.

Others concerned about the system's long-term financial viability, and its ability to provide economic security for the nation's elderly, favor raising or eliminating the cap on the earnings subject to Social Security taxes. This solution would both address the need to bring in more dollars and make the tax itself less regressive.

REGRESSIVE STATE AND LOCAL TAXES MAKE THINGS WORSE

In addition to bearing the cost of a less progressive federal tax policy, women are often the big losers at the state and local levels. While most of this volume focuses on the federal tax system, it is important to understand that state and local taxes, which obviously vary across the nation, make up a substantial portion of most households' tax bills. Since most states depend on regressive taxes like sales and excise taxes, low- and moderate-income families pay a higher share of their income to the states and localities than higher income families. In 2002, on average, the top 1 percent of tax filers paid 5.2 percent of their income in state and local taxes, while those in the bottom 20 percent paid 11.4 percent.[47] And while those earning poverty level wages usually don't earn enough to be liable for federal income taxes, 18 of the 42 states that levy state income taxes have a low enough threshold so that poor families often end up paying them.[48]

Moreover, those tax filers who itemize typically lower their federal tax payment by taking deductions for state and local income and property taxes.[49] A new provision passed in 2004 allows taxpayers to deduct for sales taxes, the highly regressive taxes that fall heavily on low- and middle-income groups, but only if they itemize their deductions and do not deduct state income taxes. Because only taxpayers who itemize their deductions can benefit, this change does not usually help those at the low end of the income scale, who tend not to itemize.[50]

Changes in state tax policies over the past fifteen years exacerbated the already regressive character of many state and local tax systems. A recent report by the Center on Budget and Policy Priorities found that during the recession of the early 1990s, many states increased taxes, with fully 46 percent of those increases coming from regressive taxes.[51] But when the recession ended and economic prosperity led to higher state revenues, cuts in state taxes targeted primarily progressive taxes like income taxes. Of the approximately $35 billion in cuts in state taxes from 1994 to 2001, only about 3 percent were net reductions in sales and excise taxes, while 81 percent were reductions in progressive taxes, mainly in personal or corporate income taxes or estate taxes.[52] So while low- and moderate-income families shouldered a disproportionate share of the tax increases in the early 1990s, tax cuts in the mid-to-late 1990s went disproportionately to higher income families.

Ronnie Steinberg, director of the Women's Social Policy and Research Center and professor of sociology at Vanderbilt University, has examined how low-income women in Tennessee, which relies almost entirely on revenue from sales tax, pay a much higher proportion of their disposable income in taxes than higher income families do.[53] In a study on how that tax policy affected women across income levels and household types, Steinberg found that a single female head-of-household earning $10,000 or less (overwhelmingly likely to be a woman of color) spent $7.14 out of every $100 she earned on sales taxes, while a husband and wife earning $113,000 spent $2.54 out of every $100 they earned on sales taxes. Also like many states, Tennessee has a constitutional amendment requiring a balanced budget. This means when state revenues fall, as during a recession, sales tax rates are likely to rise, while at the same time there is less money to pay for safety net programs. Therein lies the double whammy for low-income families: regressive state taxes take more from those with less, and inadequate states revenues, combined with balanced budget mandates, mean that states fail these same families when they face hard times.

After the economic boom in the later part of the 1990s, state fiscal crises returned with a vengeance during the recession of 2001–2003. According to the Center for Policy Alternatives, state governments have had to deal with a cumulative budget deficit of close to $200 billion since 2001, with more problems in store for many states.[54] In most states, if taxes were restored to pre-1994 levels, current budget problems would be solved.

Instead, states have faced new federal policies that both reduced state revenues and increased states' responsibilities to pick up the tab for a series of unfunded federal mandates, including the No Child Left Behind Act and Homeland Security. Many states, especially those that did not explicitly uncouple their state tax systems from the federal tax code, lost tax revenue because of the way the federal tax cuts of 2001–2003 impacted state tax collections.

In the wake of these fiscal crises, states used a combination of spending cuts and tax increases to try to close the gaping holes in their budgets. On balance, they relied more on spending cuts than tax increases. As a result, state spending in 2004, at 4.6 percent of the Gross Domestic Product, was at its lowest level in fifteen years.[55] These spending cuts have imposed significant hardships on both low- and moderate-income families. For example, 34 states cut eligibility for public health insurance, 23 states reduced eligibility for child-care subsidies, and real per-pupil aid to K–12 education fell in 34 states.[56] Cuts to public higher education have been so great that tuition increases in the double digits have resulted, curtailing access to college for students with limited resources and burdening many middle-class families with skyrocketing bills.

While state spending cuts hit programs used by most state residents, they have been particularly tough on families that lost jobs or were unable to find work during the recession. For example, during the 2001–2003 recession, a smaller proportion of poor families were able to access the new Temporary Assistance for Needy Families (TANF) welfare program than during the previous recession, when the program's predecessor, Aid to Families with Dependent Children, served as a better safety net during hard times. In fact, cash assistance through TANF or Unemployment Insurance went to only 253,000 more households in 2003 than in 2000, despite the fact that the number of poor children living in single mother homes grew by 783,000 during that time.[57] (See graph 4.2.)

Over much of the twentieth century, the federal government has been willing and able to help states meet their obligations to residents through revenue sharing and sharing the costs of joint federal-state programs. But the enormous federal tax cuts of 2001–2003, including those not yet fully phased in, promise to further decrease the funds available to help the states.

GRAPH 4.2
THE SHRINKING SAFETY NET

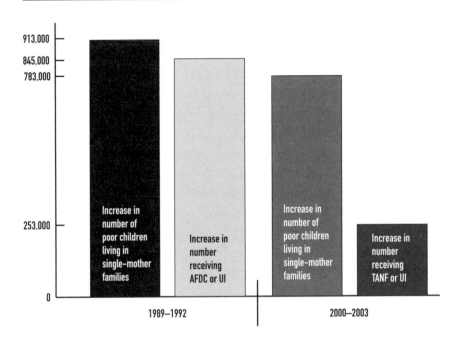

Source: Shawn Fremstad, Sharon Parrott, and Arloc Sherman (2004), *Unemployment Insurance Does Not Explain Why TANF Caseloads Are Falling as Poverty and Need are Rising* (October 12), Center on Budget and Policy Priorities: <http://www.cbpp.org/10-12-04tanf.htm>.

Ultimately, low- and moderate-income families will face a combination of more cuts in public services and potentially higher (regressive) state taxes, even as they effectively help to subsidize federal tax cuts for those at the top of the income scale.

RECENT TAX CUTS: WOMEN AND CHILDREN LAST

Since 2001, a series of massive tax cuts and changes to the tax code have intensified the trend toward less progressive tax policies. Some low- and moderate-income households have benefited modestly from some of these changes: an initial general tax rebate, a reduction to 10 percent in the rate for the lowest tax bracket, some improvements in the Child Tax Credit and the

Earned Income Tax Credit, and a change in the tax penalty for dual-earner married couples. But for the most part, the tax cuts have seriously short-changed women.

Overall, these recent tax cuts have showered most of the benefits on tax-payers with higher incomes, a group that is disproportionately White and male. According to a Congressional Budget Office analysis of the combined effects of tax cuts in 2001, 2002, and 2003, the top fifth of income earners have seen their effective tax rate drop by 3 percentage points, while rates for the lowest two-fifths have remained relatively constant.[58] In 2004, the cuts saved the richest 1 percent of Americans—whose average income is over $1.2 million per year—an average of $40,900, more than 40 times the average tax savings for middle-class taxpayers.[59] The National Women's Law Center reported that with the 2001 tax cuts initially proposed by the Bush adminis-tration, the richest 1 percent of U.S. taxpayers would have received upwards of 36 percent of the cuts, even though they paid only 20 percent of all federal taxes.[60]

Many women, on the other hand, received little or no benefit from these tax cuts. According to the National Women's Law Center's analysis—one of the few to focus specifically on women—the original 2001 proposal simply left out 27 percent of all taxpayers, most of them women. Among those excluded were families with children and incomes below 125 percent of the poverty line. Of the adults in these families, 61 percent were women—17 million in all. No tax cut would be received by 3.1 million single mothers—36 percent of all single mothers. This number included 1.3 million African American single mothers, and 630,000 Latina single mothers—almost half of the African American women and Latinas raising children as single parents. Most of the 2.8 million women living alone who had incomes below the fed-eral poverty line, including 1.5 million elderly women, were also too poor to benefit from the cuts.[61] While the tax cuts approved by Congress and ulti-mately put into effect were slightly more generous to low-income people, they still failed to benefit most of the poorest Americans, including a dispro-portionate number of women

If the tax cuts failed to reach the women most in need, they also did little for most middle-class women. George W. Bush presented his first round of tax cuts in 2001 by saying, "It is time to reward the work of people trying to enter the middle class and put some more money in their pockets at a time when they need it."[62] Three years and two more rounds of tax cuts later, the numbers told a very different story. According to figures compiled by the Center on Budget and Policy Priorities in April 2004, taxpayers with incomes in the middle 20 percent could expect to receive only 8.9 percent of 2004 tax cuts, while the top 1 percent would receive 24.2 percent. Those with incomes over $1 million alone would receive 15.3 percent of the cuts—increasing their after-tax income by 6.4 percent, compared to a 2.3 percent increase in the middle-income group. In dollar terms, the sum of 2004 tax cuts to this handful of millionaires (0.2 percent of households, or 257,000) would be nearly twice as large as the sum of cuts for the entire middle 20 percent (28.7 million households).[63] Since 2001, the three major tax bills granted an average tax cut of $647 to the middle-income group. This compares to $34,992 for the top 1 percent, and a whopping $123,592 for those with income above $1 million.[64] The tax cut for one millionaire was about five times the $23,400 annual median income for a single mother in 2004.[65]

Of course, these cuts to the federal income tax also did little for the nearly three-fourths of families who pay more in payroll taxes than income taxes[66]—or for those low- and middle-income families who pay a larger portion of their income in state and local taxes.

On the business side, recent tax cuts also bypassed many female small business owners, such as beauticians, typists, caterers, and other self-employed women with low-income operations. In describing cuts in business taxes in January 2003, President Bush declared, "Small businesses stand to gain a great deal from the tax cut plan" because 23 million small business owners would receive an average tax cut of $2,042 that year.[67] However, as Joan Entmacher of the National Women's Law Center points out, the argument "that the plan helps small business is vastly overstated."[68] The Urban-Brookings Tax Policy Center reports that 79 percent of tax filers with small business income—nearly four in five—received less than the promised amount, with most getting $500 or less. The "average" is skewed because a small number of wealthy people have some small business income, which brings the average dollar amount up.[69] In fact, 87 percent of women-owned businesses have receipts of less than $50,000, so more than a third of the 9.1 million women who own those businesses received less than $100.[70]

A PERSONAL STORY: SMALL BUSINESS FEELS THE PINCH

The sign above the door to Vickie's Place, a small restaurant in Harrison County, Ohio, welcomes locals and visitors alike to this spot where "friends meet and eat." Located in the center of a rural town across the street from its historic courthouse, Vickie's Place is the heartbeat of the community, with about 25 tables and a staff of ten, including its owner/operator and chief cook, Vickie Beetham.

While Beetham, a White, married woman, enjoys her work, she knows firsthand the difficulties of sustaining a small business. "I am increasingly worried about the instability of the 'small business' restaurant industry as a place to work. My staff—who are all local women earning low hourly wages plus tips—are seeing a large chunk of their earnings going to taxes, especially the Medicare and Social Security payroll taxes." One of Beetham's employees, who had been on welfare, now lives on the small salary she earns at the restaurant. Luckily, she is still eligible for Medicaid. But other employees and friends have not been so lucky: if they're not married to someone with family coverage, or if they don't meet the stringent requirements for Medicaid, they can find themselves saddled with large debt from medical bills, and may sometimes fail to seek medical care even when they need it.

But Beetham and her employees are not among those who benefited significantly from the Bush administration's "tax relief" legislation in 2001 and 2003. "My business was too small—we barely make a profit—so I didn't see any tax refund check as a result of the tax cuts," Beetham says. Indeed, many small businesses, like most low-income working people, got little "relief" from the tax cuts.

"As a small business owner, I'm fearful that tax policies and the lack of basic services like affordable medical care make it impossible to

ensure that my workers have a living wage. And I'm not sure that community support is enough to prevent the small-town business from becoming a thing of the past, as workers are forced to opt for the increased economic stability that might be offered by the larger chain restaurants out in the malls and at highway rest stops."

THE ALTERNATIVE MINIMUM TAX: THE "STEALTH TAX"

In 1969, Congress implemented a minimum tax to ensure that the highest income taxpayers did not take undue advantage of tax laws to reduce or eliminate their federal income tax liability. Transformed in 1982 to the Alternative Minimum Tax (AMT), this tax differs from regular income tax in several ways. While the top AMT tax rate is 28 percent on taxable income over $175,000, compared with 35 percent for regular income tax, it often applies to more of a taxpayer's income. The AMT eliminates several important deductions and other reductions to tax liability that are built into the regular income tax. For instance, under the AMT, taxable income is reduced by a large overall exemption amount (currently $58,000 for married couples and $40,250 for single taxpayers), rather than by the variety of personal exemptions and itemized deductions allowed under regular income taxes.[71] To determine whether the AMT applies to them, high-income taxpayers must calculate their tax liability twice—once under the regular income tax rules and again under the AMT rule—and pay the higher of the two tax liabilities.

Because the AMT does not index its tax rates or exemption amounts for inflation, the number and percentage of taxpayers affected by the AMT have been increasing over time. The tax cuts of 2001 and 2003 have also increased the reach and significance of the Alternative Minimum Tax (AMT). Therefore the tax, originally limited in scope and applied to only a small number of high-income households, is increasingly targeting middle-income families, especially those with dependents, and is becoming an important and growing source of federal revenue.[72]

In 1990, only 132,000 wealthy people paid the AMT.[73] By 1995, 414,000 paid, and in 2000, that number was up to 1.3 million, about 1 percent of all taxpayers.[74] In 2005, the AMT will affect roughly 3 percent of taxpayers. But if the tax code is left unchanged, it is anticipated that by 2010, more than 20 percent of all taxpayers—some 30 million Americans—will pay the AMT.[75] In other words, in just five years, the AMT will be paid by the majority of taxpayers with adjusted gross incomes of between $50,000 and $100,000.[76] In contrast, more than two-thirds of taxpayers with incomes greater than $500,000 will *not* be affected by the AMT because they already face the nation's highest effective tax rates under the regular income tax system.[77]

With its few exemptions, the AMT also imposes a strict marriage penalty. The Urban-Brookings Tax Policy Center found that married households will be more than twenty times as likely as singles to face the AMT in 2010.[78] Moreover, because the AMT prohibits deductions for dependents, 85 percent of all married couples with two or more children will be hit by the AMT in 2010; and among married couples with two children who earn between $75,000 and $100,000, that number rises to 97 percent.[79]

As the AMT begins to affect people with lower incomes, women increasingly bear the brunt of the tax. The AMT has even hit some people making under $30,000.[80] Less than one in 2,000 in that lower-income group fell under the AMT in 2002. But by 2010, the number will increase fourfold, to one in 500—about 130,000 families in all, many of them headed by single women. David Cay Johnston notes the significance for women: "Single mothers head many of these families. These women, some widows and others divorced, already have to cope with a modest income, rearing children, and a property tax bill on the family home if they are lucky enough to own one. Now they will lose some or all of their tax cuts to make sure that people making $1 million or more can pay less tax."[81]

The growing reach of the AMT reflects two key factors. Unlike the regular income tax, the AMT suffers from "bracket creep." The growth of the economy plus inflation naturally causes a steady increase in taxpayer incomes—along with a similar increase in the cost of living. But the AMT is not indexed for inflation. This mean that as incomes rise along with inflation, the AMT's standard deduction shrinks in relative terms, and more middle-income taxpayers become subject to the AMT, even though their buying power, in real terms, has not grown.[82] At the same time, since taxpayers must pay the greater of either their AMT or regular tax liability, the 2001 and 2003 tax cuts also pushed more taxpayers into the AMT bracket. Together, these trends have made the AMT the fastest growing tax on middle- and upper-middle class families.[83]

Congress and the president have chosen not to modify the AMT to reduce its impact on the middle class, in part because the tax has helped fill the revenue gap created by the recent tax cuts. In 2001, the AMT raised only 1 percent of income tax revenue,[84] but by 2010, economists predict it will be responsible for 10 percent of income tax revenues[85]—enough to offset monies lost to the tax cuts.[86] These added dollars make it difficult to eliminate or reduce the AMT. Its repeal would deprive the Treasury of $790 billion from 2006 through 2015, including increased interest on the debt, which would rise with the decrease in tax revenues—and even more if the 2001 and 2003 tax cuts are extended.[87] Some projections conclude that the cost of removing the AMT would be higher than the cost of removing the individual income tax itself by 2008.[88]

Some tax analysts have suggested that Congress could preserve revenue levels while shifting the focus of the AMT from the middle class and back onto higher-income taxpayers. This might be achieved by indexing AMT tax brackets to inflation, increasing deductions for dependents, and making it harder for the rich to shelter income from taxes.[89] Whatever the solution, reform of the AMT should restore the original purpose of the tax, that is, to ensure that the richest taxpayers pay their fair share, and not add to the overall tax bills of those in the middle- or low-income range.

THE END RESULT: WHERE THE TAX SYSTEM WORKS

This chapter describes how the overall tax system has become generally less progressive. But there are also some bright spots in current tax policy.

For example, the federal income tax, as a progressive tax, is one that works for most women. With a lower tax rate for those in the lowest income bracket, with a relatively generous tax break for single heads-of-households, with credits for children and deductions for child-care expenses, the income tax helps low- and middle-income women maintain financial independence and balance their work and family responsibilities.

Another of those bright spots has been the expansion of the Earned Income Tax Credit (EITC), a huge source of tax relief—and even positive income—for low-income women. Instituted to compensate low-income people for payroll tax increases, the EITC was significantly expanded in 1996 to help ensure that it achieved that goal. One of the reasons it is so valuable, both at the federal level and in states that have a refundable EITC, is the fact that it provides income in the form of a refund to those who need it most—workers with incomes so low that the credit is larger than the taxes owed.

This change, like other positive policies for women and children, didn't just happen. Advocates for women and fair taxes, including many of the Council's member centers, continue to fight hard for such reforms. Defending and expanding the EITC and its refundability is a crucial policy objective that will help women maintain their families.

AND WHERE THE SYSTEM DOESN'T WORK: LESS BANG FOR THE BUCK

Despite these few bright spots, the overall trend in recent tax policy has been toward a less progressive tax system. This trend is not new. Begun in the 1970s and accelerated during the Reagan administration, it has continued under almost every administration since then. President George H. W. Bush famously declared, "Read my lips: No new taxes." President Bill Clinton declared that "the era of big government is over." And President George W. Bush has advocated for some of the deepest tax cuts in the nation's history for wealthy individuals and businesses.

The underlying, but contested, rationale driving this tax policy is that economic growth is best served by increasing the role of the private market and downsizing the role of government. In 2004, the conservative Heritage Foundation claimed that "the [2003 tax cut] legislation had much to do with the timing of economic take-off. American companies responded to the 2003 tax cuts by employing more workers and investing in more capital equipment almost the moment lower taxes became law."[90] But, in fact, job growth in 2003 lagged below average numbers needed for recovery, and the average size of the labor force was only 0.6 percent larger in 2004.[91]

According to Mark Zandi, chief economist of the independent research firm Economy.com, the latest tax cuts produced very little bang for the buck: they yielded less than one dollar of short-term economic demand for each one dollar of cost. A stimulus package that favored low- and middle-income taxpayers—those most likely to spend the extra money—would have done a better job.[92] A 2004 analysis by the International Monetary Fund states, "The recent emphasis on cutting taxes, boosting defense and security outlays, and spurring an economic recovery may come at the eventual cost of upward pressure on interest rates, a crowding out of private investment, and an erosion of longer-term US productivity growth."[93] And a report from the group United for a Fair Economy observes, "History shows that large tax giveaways for the rich and extreme inequality of wealth are followed by weak economic growth and job loss."[94]

Finally, despite the small-government rhetoric, government has not become smaller. Overall government spending has grown, and in the absence of adequate revenue, the national debt has grown as well. What has shrunk is the funding for government services for the basic functions of our society—services that promote economic security, a healthy and educated populace, public safety, equitable opportunity, and essential support for the most disadvantaged among us.

HOW DOES ALL THIS ADD UP FOR WOMEN?

As tax policy, and especially the recent cuts, reduce the proportion of the tax bill paid by higher-income households and large corporations, moderate- and lower-income households and smaller businesses shoulder a growing share of the cost of public services. It is no wonder that many voters have been susceptible to the promises of politicians to lower, or not raise, taxes. Yet many of these voters have enjoyed little or no significant savings to their tax bills. And many more—including most women—recognize the importance of public programs that help them and their neighbors live safe and productive lives, and weather hardships and uncertainties. Women today are positioned at the convergence of a tax system that is less and less progressive and a public funding system whose coffers have been drained of the revenues necessary to promote their economic security and opportunity.

But it does not have to be this way. A truly fair tax policy can reverse the trend toward overtaxing moderate- and low-income families—a trend that severely disadvantages women—while still ensuring sufficient revenue to sustain the public services, programs, and resources necessary for our families and our country to flourish.

STRAIGHT TALK ABOUT WOMEN AND TAXES: HOW TO MAKE THE CASE

To those who say: We're all better off when those with wealth keep more of their money so they can invest it. The benefits of those investments "trickle down" to those at the bottom of the economic scale.

We say: What's really trickled down to those with middle and lower incomes—including most women—has been a relatively greater share of the tax bill. The cost of government spending is increasingly being shifted away from wealthy individuals and corporations and more onto those who depend on wages and government services for their well-being.

- We're relying less and less on progressive taxes like the federal income tax that leave more after-tax income in the pockets of middle- and lower-income women than flat or regressive taxes do. And even income tax rates have gotten less progressive. Do we really want to make those who have the least in our society pay more of the nation's tax bill?
- We're cutting taxes on wealth, like the estate tax and the capital gains tax. Do we really want people who earn a substantial amount of their yearly income from stock dividends to pay a lower tax rate on that income than those whose only earnings comes from work?
- We're also cutting corporate taxes. Do we really want corporations paying the lowest percentage of earnings against GDP ever, while our national debt continues to grow?
- Wealthy individuals and corporations depend upon public services like education, infrastructure, and homeland security to provide stability and

create the conditions for their own financial success. Don't we want to be sure they pay their fair share toward the cost of these services?

- "Tax relief" is an appealing misnomer. Instead of bringing relief, those cuts have just shifted the costs down—down to the state and local levels, down to those with middle and lower incomes, and down to women, who often have to pick up the care-giving work as programs are cut. Is this the kind of "reform" we really want for our tax system?

5 | HOW TODAY'S POLICIES HURT WOMEN, CHILDREN, AND FAMILIES

Working through our government, we have a responsibility to fund critical public services and to provide aid for the poorest and most vulnerable populations. The current tax and budget system is broken—the tax system is unfair, and the total revenues raised are inadequate. The solution is not just to forget about it. Major reforms in taxes and public policies are absolutely necessary.

— *Heidi Hartmann, President, Institute for Women's Policy Research[1]*

Who wins and who loses as the U.S. tax system changes? Data show that over the last 30 years, the cost of public services has shifted more from families with high incomes to those with lower incomes, from corporations to individuals, from wealth to work, and from federal to state and city governments. As the tax system has grown less progressive and two rounds of tax cuts have reduced revenues, the nation faces increasing economic challenges: deep budget cuts, a growing gap between rich and poor, reduced public services, record deficits, and a ballooning debt. These changes fall heavily on women and pose a serious threat to the future of public services—and not just those for the poor.

THE SHIFT IN THE TAX BILL HURTS WOMEN

While affluent groups still pay higher income taxes, their relative share has declined at a much greater rate, especially in the last four years, than the share for low- and moderate- income families, where women predominate. Between 1979 and 2000, the share of pretax income (adjusted for inflation) nearly doubled for the top 1 percent of earners, while it dropped for the bottom 80 percent of earners. Yet during that same period, the effective federal tax rate for the top 1 percent fell from 37 percent to 33.2 percent, and their after-tax income tripled.[2]

Other shifts have also had an impact. The individual income tax, which is still relatively progressive, has remained a steady percentage of total federal revenues, while the share contributed by corporate taxes, another progressive tax, has sharply declined. Corporate income and excise taxes have shrunk since 1946 from about half of all federal tax revenue to less than 15 percent. And payroll taxes—which, as currently structured, fall heaviest on lower- and moderate- income workers, including large numbers of women—have significantly increased, from about 10 percent to more than a third of revenues.[3] If current trends continue, some economists predict that more than half of all federal revenue will come from the payroll tax within the next decade.[4]

Tax cuts enacted in 2001 and 2003 have accelerated this trend. According to Citizens for Tax Justice, the tax cuts lowered the combined federal, state, and local tax rate for the top 1 percent of taxpayers by 12 percent, while middle- and low-income taxpayers enjoyed cuts of only 7 and 3 percent respectively.[5]

GRAPH 5.1
TYPE OF TAX AS A SHARE OF FEDERAL REVENUES, 1946–2004

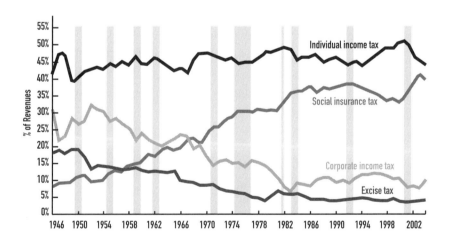

Source: Urban-Brookings Tax Policy Center (2004), *Tax Facts*, Overview/Composition of Taxes: <http://www.tax-policycenter.org/TaxFacts/Tfdb/TFTemplate.cfm?DocID=264&Topic2id=20&Topic3id=21>. Reproduced from Adam Carcasso, "The Corporate Income Tax in the Post-War Era," Tax Facts Column, *Tax Notes Magazine*, 3 March 2003. Based on data from Budget of the United States Government, FY 2006.

WHILE THE RICH GET RICHER, MOST WOMEN DON'T

The effect of a particular tax on a household's after-tax income is one of the most reliable ways to measure the fairness of that tax. Applying this criteria, it is clear that the benefits yielded by the last 25 years of tax policy have not been equally shared. Instead, the rich have experienced enormous growth in after-tax income, while the poor and even the middle classes have experienced only negligible to moderate growth. This is thanks, in part, to changes to the tax code, which leave more and more of the largest incomes intact while increasing the tax bill for low and moderate incomes. In fact, by 2003, the top 5 percent of the population (or 5.6 million households) received double the share of the country's income received by the entire bottom 40 percent (or 44.8 million households).

During the 1980s, changes in economic forces, including tax policy, accelerated a growth in income inequality. Despite a slight reversal of this trend during the 1990s, when such changes as the expansion of the Earned Income Tax Credit (EITC) and the Child Tax Credit (CTC) helped slow the growth in income disparity,[6] the overall trend continued over the next two decades. Between 1979 and 2002, the after-tax income of the top 1 percent of U.S. households soared by 111 percent (or $332,800), with the top 20 percent growing by 48 percent (or $42,300). In contrast, the after-tax income of taxpayers in the bottom 20 percent grew by a mere 5 percent.[7] (See graph 5.2.)

The tax cuts of 2001–2003 widened the gap in income growth. The Center on Budget and Policy Priorities, using data from the Congressional Budget Office, found that in 2004, those in the top 20 percent enjoyed a 3.3 percentage increase in after-tax income, compared with a 1.5 percent increase for those in the bottom 20 percent, and a 2 percent increase for those in the middle. Within the top 20 percent, the top 1 percent saw by far the largest increase—5.3 percent.[8] These inequities in income growth—and in household income—will only increase after 2005, because most of the tax cuts benefiting low- and middle-income families have been implemented, while those for the wealthy, such as the decrease and possible elimination of the estate tax, are yet to be fully phased in.

Proponents of huge tax cuts of this kind often point to the growing tax bills paid by the wealthiest taxpayers as evidence that the tax system is treat-

GRAPH 5.2
CHANGE IN AVERAGE AFTER-TAX INCOME, 1979–2002

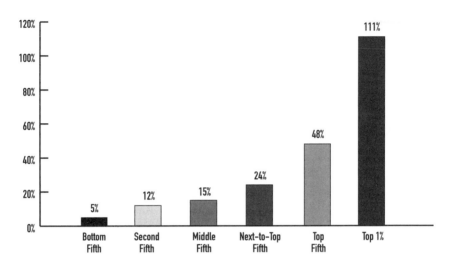

Source: Isaac Shapiro (2005), *What New CBO Data Indicate About Long-term Income Distribution Trends* (March 7), Center on Budget and Policy Priorities: <http://www.cbpp.org/3-7-05tax.htm>. Based on data from the Congressional Budget Office.

ing them unfairly. But data from the Congressional Budget Office indicate that any increase in taxes for those taxpayers results primarily from the enormous growth in their income, not from tax increases. The average tax rate on the top 1 percent of taxpayers in 2000 was lower than it had been in 1979.[9] The subsequent tax cuts only further reduced the already shrinking share of income tax paid by the richest Americans

This exponential growth for incomes at the top in comparison to incomes at the bottom has not always been the trend. From the close of World War II through 1973, the growth in family income for all economic groups was fairly equal, with those at the bottom increasing the most and those at the top the least. But from 1973 to 2000, the rate of income growth increased dramatically for those at the top, with the family income of the top earners increasing by 66.9 percent compared to only 12.1 percent of the income of the lowest earners. (See graphs 5.3 and 5.4.)

GRAPH 5.3
REAL FAMILY INCOME GROWTH, 1947–1973

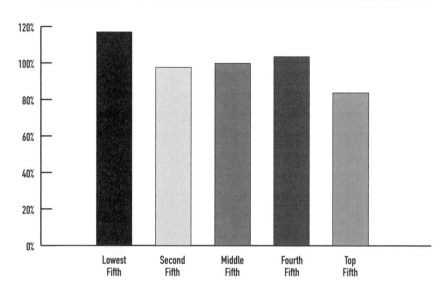

GRAPH 5.4
REAL FAMILY INCOME GROWTH, 1973–2000

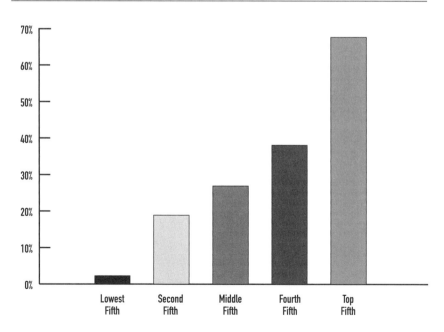

Source: Lawrence Mishel, Jared Bernstein, and Sylvia Allegretto (2005), *The State of Working America, 2004–2005* (Ithaca, N.Y.: Cornell University Press), 71.

This growth peaked in 2000, along with the stock market. Despite a subsequent drop, in 2002 the richest 1 percent of households still received a larger share of the national income than at any time since 1937, except for 1988 and the years from 1997 to 2001.[10] In 2004, following the Bush administration's tax cuts and well into the economic recovery, income inequality reached the highest levels on record. While the rich once again got richer, lower- and middle-income workers were moving in the other direction, despite the recovery. Between 2003 and 2004, the median income of working-age Americans declined, while the number living in poverty increased by 1.1 million.[11]

ROOM AT THE TOP: THE INCREASING CONCENTRATION OF INDIVIDUAL WEALTH

Instead of exerting even a mild corrective to the unprecedented growth in income disparities, U.S. tax policy in the last 25 years has only exacerbated the inequities. Except for the dwindling federal estate tax, levied when assets are transferred to heirs, the United States, for the most part, only taxes *income* produced by wealth—capital gains, dividends, and interest—and not wealth itself. But even this income from wealth is generally taxed at a lower rate than income from work. So it is not surprising that the wealthy have become more affluent in recent decades, with the richest 20 percent of households owning 83 percent of the country's assets in 2001.[12] (See graph 5.5.)

When viewed through a racial and gendered lens, this growing wealth gap is even more stark. The average female-headed household in 2001 had a net worth of $27,850, compared to an average of $86,100 for all U.S. households.[13] And nearly 31 percent of African American households had zero or a negative net worth, that is they had no assets like savings accounts, property, or pensions and in some cases, even owed money, compared to about 13 percent of White households.[14]

GRAPH 5.5
DISTRIBUTION OF WEALTH IN THE UNITED STATES, 2001

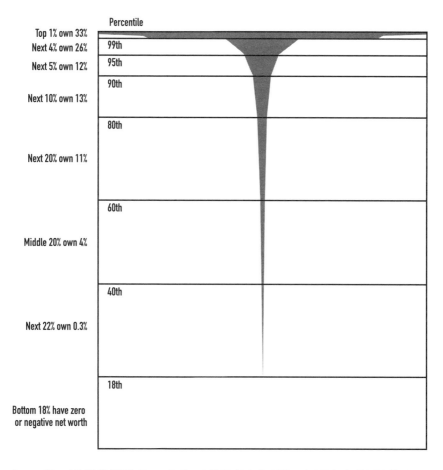

Source: Edward N. Wolff (2004), *Changes in Household Wealth in the 1980s and 1990s in the U.S.*, Working Paper No. 407 (May), Levy Economics Institute of Bard College: <http://www.levy.org/default.asp?view=publications_view&pubID=fca3a440ee>.

LESS GOVERNMENT MONEY MEANS FEWER PUBLIC GOODS AND RISING PUBLIC DEBT

The income and wealth produced by three decades of supply-side tax and spending policies have failed to "trickle down" to women and other middle- and low-income households. The policies have not led to more jobs, less

poverty, and a diminished need for the welfare state as supply-siders promised. Instead, tax policy during the last 30 years, and especially in the last four
years has not only increased the gap between the rich and the poor but also
decreased federal revenues, generated growing federal budget deficits,
thrown the nation deeper into debt, strained many state and local budgets,
and reduced resources available for spending on public goods and services on
which many women and their families depend.

Decreased Federal Revenues. After World War II, federal tax revenues, measured as a percentage of the Gross Domestic Product (GDP), rose rather
steadily from 14.4 percent of GDP in 1950 to a high of 19.7 percent of GDP
in the late 1960s. For the next three decades, total revenues fluctuated from a
low of 17.3 percent of GDP in 1971 to a new high of 20.9 percent in 2000.
Since then, in the wake of massive tax cuts in 2001 and 2003, revenues
dropped to an estimated 15.8 percent of GDP in 2004, the lowest level since
1950.[15] The Center on Budget and Policy Priorities reports that if the 2001
and 2003 tax cuts are made permanent, they will cost a total of $5.1 trillion in
decreased federal revenues and increased interest costs through 2015—an
amount of money more than three times the budgets for all federal education programs or for all veterans' programs and more than 30 times greater
than the budget of the Environment Protection Agency.[16] Speaking in 2004,
the National Women's Law Center's Joan Entmacher put government revenue cuts in dramatic context: "Federal revenues this year are at the lowest
level of the share of the economy since 1950. We are back to the future. For
those of you who don't remember the fifties . . . there was no Medicare. There
was no Medicaid. There was no Department of Education. There was no
Department of Housing and Urban Development. There wasn't even an
interstate highway system, for better or worse. It was a very different place."[17]

Larger Deficits. During the years following World War II, rising tax revenues
typically covered the nation's costs, with minimal deficits used to stimulate
the economy. But following the military buildup and tax cuts of the Reagan
years, mounting deficits led to a drive to balance the budget, largely through
cutting social programs. Those budget cuts, along with tax increases and a

period of strong economic growth, led to budget surpluses at the end of the 1990s, which in 2001 the U.S. Treasury predicted would reach $5 trillion within the decade. Women and many others had high hopes that renewed spending would restore needed benefits and services. Instead, Congress passed another round of tax cuts. Rather than supporting domestic programs or paying down the national debt, the new tax policies combined with ballooning military expenditures to produce record deficits in the federal budget. In 2004, the deficit rose to $413 billion. For the first time since World War II, the deficit had grown four years in a row.[18] At 4.2 percent of GDP, the current deficit represents a larger share of the economy than the combined spending of the Departments of Education, Homeland Security, Interior, Justice, and State.[19] Ongoing deficits threaten the long-term health of the U.S. economy by reducing savings and investment and slowing economic growth.

Deeper in Debt. Like the rest of us, when the government lacks the funds needed to pay its bills, it borrows. The tax cuts, and the annual deficits they produce, have also plunged the nation deeper into debt. Now $7.4 trillion[20] (including what is owed to the Social Security Trust Fund), the national debt will reach $9.1 trillion (51 percent of GDP) in 2014 under current policies, according to estimates by the Center on Budget and Policy Priorities.[21] At $318 billion in 2003, interest payments on the national debt—owed to foreign nations, large banks, major corporations, and wealthy individuals—amount to the third largest item in the federal budget, draining revenue badly needed to pay for critical programs.

Less Federal Spending. Paralleling the drop in tax revenues, total federal spending declined steadily from 23.5 percent of GDP in the early Reagan years to 18.6 percent of GDP by 2003—the same level as in 1963, before the Great Society programs of the late 1960s, which were designed to reduce poverty and equalize opportunity.[22]

Over the last 25 years, *domestic discretionary spending* decreased steadily, from a high of 4.8 percent of GDP in 1978 to 3.4 percent in 2004.[23] Domestic discretionary spending includes nonmilitary and noninternational programs like education, human services, and transportation, over which Congress has considerable control. To cut spending, Congress tightened eligibility for programs, lowered benefit levels, or transferred responsibility for the program from the federal government to states or the private sector. Current plans, including the administration's proposed budget for 2006, call for additional cuts in nearly all domestic programs—and women and children will be the big losers, especially in communities of color and among the poor. (See graph 5.6.) To put these cuts in context, Richard Kogan and David Kamin of the Center on Budget and Policy Priorities state: "The savings in 2005 through 2009 from all of the domestic discretionary cuts combined would be substantially less than the cost in those years of the income tax cuts just for the one percent of households with the highest incomes."[24]

GRAPH 5.6
DISCRETIONARY SPENDING AS A PERCENTAGE OF GDP, 1963–2009

Source: Isaac Shapiro and David Kamin (2004), *Concentrating on the Wrong Target: Bush Cuts Would Reduce Domestic Discretionary Spending as a Share of GDP to Its Lowest Level in 46 Years* (March 5), Center for Budget and Policy Priorities: <http://www.cbpp.org/2-27-04bud.htm>. Based on data from the U.S. Office of Management and Budget and Congressional Budget Office.

Unlike discretionary spending, *mandatory spending* for entitlement programs like Social Security and Medicare is guaranteed by federal law and is thus less vulnerable to budget cuts. However, in 1996, welfare lost its status as an entitlement to individuals altogether. And with proposals being floated to privatize Social Security and Medicare, the entitlement status of even these programs is at risk. The total dollar figure for the cost of entitlement programs continues to rise because of population growth and other factors. Spending for Medicare and Medicaid also continues to grow as a share of GDP, due to rising health care costs. However, spending on Social Security as a percentage of GDP has fallen from 4.9 percent in 1983 to 3.4 percent in 2004.

A LOSE-LOSE FORMULA FOR WOMEN

The current fiscal situation leaves women and families in a lose-lose situation. The growth in government spending—especially for debt service, the military, and entitlement programs like Medicare—is on a collision course with the decrease in federal revenues that resulted from the 2001 and 2003 tax cuts. Unless Congress reverses the tax cuts or reduces the huge increases in military spending (or both), the nation faces three possible scenarios, all of which would have negative effects on everyone, but especially on women and other vulnerable populations.

The first possibility is *large deficit spending*—that is, we continue to finance current programs through borrowing and continue to grow the national debt, leading to rising interest rates, decreased national savings, and most likely, long-term economic contraction.

The second scenario sees *cuts to mandatory spending* for entitlement programs, starting with Medicaid, but also Social Security and other universal programs, all of which disproportionately serve women and their children.

And the third option is continued—and increasing—*cuts to discretionary programs* like education, transportation, or medical research. Heidi Hartmann of the Institute for Women's Policy Research explains that while the government has made a commitment to supporting entitlement programs and has promised to cut taxes for the wealthiest citizens, there seems to be no plan for how we are going to support important programs such as Head Start, housing assistance, or job-training programs.[25] In fact, if current tax and spending policies remain in place, overall funding by 2009 for domestic discretionary programs (not including Homeland Security) is projected to be $45.4 billion—10.4 percent below the level needed to keep up with inflation.[26] At 2.6 percent of the GDP, this will represent the smallest share of the economy since 1963.[27] And things could get even worse. According to C. Eugene Steuerle of the Urban Institute, "If the budget simply were balanced, and recent tax cuts and spending increases were made permanent, then existing commitments would totally wipe out other domestic outlays by 2012."[28] Rising spending and declining receipts would leave no funding at all for discretionary programs. (See graph 5.7.)

GRAPH 5.7
DISAPPEARING FUNDS FOR DOMESTIC DISCRETIONARY PROGRAMS

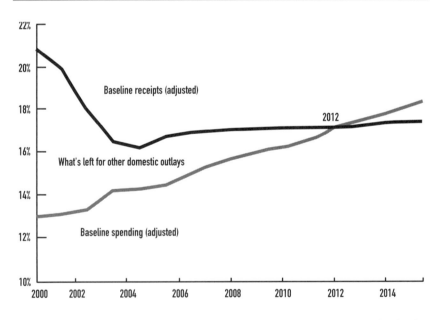

Source: C. Eugene Steuerle, Adam Carasso, and Meghan Bishop (2003). Urban Institute. Projections based on data from U.S. Office of Management and Budget and Congressional Budget Office. From Eugene C. Steuerle (2003). *The Incredible Shrinking Budget for Working Families and Children*, The Urban Institute: <http://www.urban.org/url.cfm?ID=310914>.

While it is highly unlikely that *all* discretionary or entitlement spending will be cut, or that huge, unlimited deficits will be tolerated, these projections make it clear that the big squeeze is very real. Whatever combination of deficit spending, program cuts, and revenue increases policymakers impose, tax reform must first and foremost address this crisis, by enhancing the progressivity of the entire tax system and ensuring adequate tax revenues for the full range of public programs that contribute to economic and national security.

The trajectory produced by our current tax policy has real consequences for women, who rely more on those very programs and protections that are feeling the squeeze. When legislators are unwilling to buck the anti-tax, small government rhetoric that so dominates our political discourse, then they are forced to cut domestic programs—as they have done, repeatedly, over the last several decades. Those who most need those publicly funded social services—disproportionately women and children—often have less political clout, so the trend continues. The programs that support these vulnerable populations will be especially at risk of additional cuts in the future.

STRAIGHT TALK ABOUT WOMEN AND TAXES: HOW TO MAKE THE CASE

To those who say: We may need to make some adjustments, but we all benefit when taxes are cut and the size of government shrinks.

We say: The benefits of changes in tax policy over the last three decades have gone mainly to the wealthy, leaving most women seriously shortchanged.

- The after-tax income of those with the highest incomes has grown by huge percentages in the last 25 years: it's more than doubled for the top 1 percent of the population. For those in the middle, income growth has been only 15 percent, and for the lowest fifth of the population, a mere 5 percent.
- Tax policies are partly responsible for the gap in income growth, and the widening gap between the rich and the poor. Increasingly, we are a society made up of the very rich and then all the rest: in 2001, the richest 20 percent of households owned 83 percent of the country's assets.

- With recent tax cuts, we are running huge annual deficits, and our national debt has ballooned. Now at over $7 trillion (including about $3 trillion owed to the Social Security Trust Fund), the debt is expected to reach more than $9 trillion by 2014. We are going to pay for that, through increased interest payments on the debt. Already, in 2005, we're paying almost 19 percent of our federal budget on interest, while only about 3 percent is going to education. And ultimately, our children and grandchildren will foot the bill!
- We're all hurt when there's not enough money to fund necessary public services, like education and homeland security—but women are especially hurt when programs that provide support for them and their families are cash-starved.

6 | WHY WOMEN FEEL MORE STING FROM SERVICE CUTS

Our country encourages people to improve themselves and work hard to achieve the American Dream. But the current federal policy environment does little to support those efforts. Many programs to assist individuals with self-improvement could not serve all who were eligible and seeking services, even before tax cuts placed additional constraints on program funding for education, training, health care and related programs. Women of color tend to have greater need for these programs and they need to understand policies that reduce taxes for others may lead to less opportunity for them. The general public needs to realize that there is no such thing as a "free lunch"—lower taxes lead to fewer programs that can improve the lives of people they care about.

—Margaret C. Simms, Vice President for Governance and Economic Analysis, Joint Center for Political and Economic Studies

Discussions of tax policy usually focus on only half of the picture—paying taxes. But during the past 30 years, tax changes and tax cuts have translated into significant changes to the other side of the picture—how we use tax funds. Unwilling to raise taxes and faced with depleted revenues, many of our nation's leaders have called for government reduction and retrenchment—and have singled out many of the programs that hold special importance for women. When federal tax revenues are inadequate, social services are underfunded, cut, devolved to local levels of government, or privatized—and women and their children, who are most reliant on those programs, lose access to support, services, and protections.

But the polls tell us that many fear the impact of decreasing tax revenues and the pressure on publicly supported programs. A 2002 survey conducted by *More* magazine and Intuit showed that "women have clear opinions about how they want to see their tax dollars spent. When asked which programs they would most like to see their federal tax dollars spent on, the majority answered Social Security/Medicare (40 percent) and education (39 percent).

In actuality, about 41 percent of federal money is currently spent on Social Security/Medicare, but only 2 percent goes to education, which is largely funded at the state and local levels."[1] In an April 2003 survey of the general population, 68 percent of those polled said that they preferred that the nation spend more on domestic programs such as education, health care, and Social Security, compared with 29 percent who favored tax cuts.[2] A 2004 survey found similar preferences among Latinos, about 75 percent of whom thought the government spent too little on education and health insurance.[3] Not surprisingly, women are less likely to support tax cuts than men.[4] In a 2005 poll commissioned by the National Council for Research on Women, 46 percent of women said their families had been hurt a lot or some by cuts to government services, while only 34 percent of men held this view.[5] These spending cuts in critical areas leave needs unmet and force women—traditionally society's care-givers—to pick up the slack.

WHAT'S HAPPENING TO PUBLICLY FUNDED SERVICES THAT ARE ESPECIALLY IMPORTANT TO WOMEN?

When the Bough Breaks: Child Care. The need for quality child-care is a daily concern for the vast majority of mothers who are in the paid labor force:, 65 percent of whom have preschool children and 78 percent have school-age children.[6]

Child-care and after-school programs shape the way children think, learn, and behave well into adulthood. After-school programs are needed particularly to serve the more than 28 million children between the ages of six and seventeen from households without stay-at-home mothers or fathers.[7] By promoting a more productive workforce, facilitating school retention, and contributing to economic growth, the programs additionally benefit employers and the wider society.[8]

But despite enormous benefits, these programs face the budget ax. As a growing number of states turn away children from child-care programs, place them on waiting lists, or tighten income restrictions, only one in seven eligible children is being served.[9] Under President Bush's 2006 budget proposal, federal funding for child-care would be frozen for the fourth year in a row. By 2009, as more funds are cut and costs rise, child-care programs will serve some 300,000 fewer low-income children.[10]

Funding would also be frozen for *Head Start*, although over half of local programs have already had to cut staff and/or programs since 2002.[11] The 900,000 low-income children enrolled in Head Start represent a mere 3 percent of eligible infants and toddlers and only 60 percent of eligible preschoolers. Sarah Greene, president and CEO of the National Head Start Association, says: "What we are seeing is that you don't have to dismantle Head Start through block granting to the states to effectively undermine this fine program serving America's most at-risk children. Inadequate funding is slowly forcing programs to alter and, in some cases, kill services and teacher positions that otherwise would make a real difference in the lives of Head Start children."[12]

Not Making the Grade: Education. While states struggle to adequately fund *public education*, the President's 2006 budget proposes terminating 48 programs, including funds to states for educational technology, drug-free schools, programs to reduce alcohol abuse among students, family literacy programs, student loans, and much more.[13] In fact, nearly one-third of the domestic programs slated for cuts under this budget are in education, totaling almost $1.3 billion.[14]

To achieve a net reduction in Department of Education funding, President Bush proposes to cut billions from *college preparatory programs* for economically disadvantaged students and from *vocational education programs* that improve women's access to nontraditional occupations and increase their ability to support themselves and their families later in life.[15]

Cuts in *programs to curb dropout rates* will hit African American and Latino communities especially hard: 12 percent of African American teens and 21 percent of Latino teens currently do not finish high school.[16] The 2006 budget proposed by the President will freeze the maximum *Pell Grant* (at $4,050 per year), the basic federal program to make college affordable, for a third year in a row. In a time of rising tuition costs, a freeze is in effect a cut. The freeze on Pell Grants and on *Federal Work-Study* opportunities falls especially hard on women, who now outnumber men as college students.[17]

The budget proposal also contains a 64 percent cut in funds supporting programs for nursing students and other *training in the health professions*, a field where women predominate.[18]

A PERSONAL STORY: WHERE'S THE EQUAL OPPORTUNITY?

Avis Jones-DeWeever is a full-time, professional researcher with a Ph.D. in political science—and two sons under the age of ten. As young African American professionals, she and her husband were committed to their Washington, D.C., neighborhood, their co-op apartment, and to the concept of public education.

But when her older son, Guy, was almost ready for school, Jones-DeWeever was the one who learned a lesson. "We as a nation speak eloquently about equality of opportunity, but all you have to do is look at our school systems to know that we're not living up to our values!" "Public" education is really "local" education, to a great extent supported and limited by the resources of the immediate community, usually through property taxes and less formally through parent support and the local economy. And in the nation's capital, where 20.2 percent of the population and 31.1 percent of children live below the poverty line, public education is in bad shape, with teachers lacking the resources to overcome the substandard facilities and the challenges of inner-city education.

So despite their commitment to public education, Jones-DeWeever and her husband did what many parents feel they must do: put the interests of their child first. At first they were able to get around the abysmal conditions of the local schools by sending Guy to a private school. But with their second child on the way, they had to confront the cost of child-care as well as private school tuition—both after-tax expenses that even their two-income family couldn't afford. So they began their quest for a good public school—which, for them, meant moving to a new home in a different community.

Avis Jones-DeWeever was lucky—she was a professional researcher and she knew schools. So a year later, after spending as much as a day a week researching area schools, the family settled into a house in Prince William County, Virginia—not quite the house they wanted, and a stretch for their budget, but a house in a good school district.

Jones-DeWeever is painfully aware that many families can't make the same choice. And she knows the consequences can last a lifetime for many children who live in communities without an adequate tax base to ensure quality public services. "Leaving aside the obvious injustice of inequitable opportunity," Jones-DeWeever notes, society as a whole loses. "We must develop a workforce capable of leading the global marketplace of the future. We need to make sure all of our kids are educated and equipped with the lifelong learning skills that will enable them to contribute their energies and their smarts to our society."

A Sickening Dilemma: Health Care. Forty-five million, eight hundred thousand Americans, about one in six, lacked health insurance coverage in 2004—the largest number since the Census Bureau began reporting this data.[19] Women are more likely to lack employment-based insurance, in part because their labor participation is often interrupted or part-time due to unpaid family care-giving responsibilities. This employment-based coverage is subsidized under the fiscal welfare system—so women miss out on an important publicly supported benefit. In 2002, 18 percent of working-age women (ages 18 to 64) were uninsured by either employers or the government.[20]

The proportion of those without health insurance rose more sharply among women than men between 2002 and 2003 (4 percent compared with 1 percent); 21.2 million women and girls went without coverage. In 2004, the number of uninsured women rose again by 120,000, for a total increase of 2.3 million since 2000.[21]

Compared to Whites at 11.3 percent, larger proportions of Latinos (32.7), African Americans (19.7), and Asian Americans (16.8) live without insurance,[22] as do 45 percent of all non-citizen immigrants.[23] Children's Defense Fund figures show that nationwide, Native Americans get only 52 percent of their health needs funded.[24] Despite this vulnerability, funding for the *Office of Minority Health* would be cut by 15 percent, and the *Minority HIV/AIDS* budget along with that of the *Office on Women's Health*, would be frozen under the president's proposed budget for FY 2006.[25]

Some 60 percent of Americans who receive direct, tax-supported health care coverage under *Medicaid* are women or girls.[26] In 2001, nearly 16 million low-income women (ages 19 to 64) who are parents, pregnant, or have disabilities, got to see a doctor because Medicaid paid the bill.[27] Medicaid also covers the majority of elderly people being cared for in long-term nursing facilities. Women make up both the majority of residents in these facilities, as well as the longest-staying residents.[28] In general, states cover 25 to 50 percent of their populations' Medicaid costs while the federal government picks up the rest of the tab. Cash-strapped states have been forced to restrict services and add new copayments. Some states are trying to eliminate the entitlement to Medicaid altogether for large groups of beneficiaries, including children. The shortfalls will continue—and increase—if the 2006 federal budget proposal stands, draining $60 billion out of Medicaid over ten years.

Medicare, the publicly supported health insurance program for those 65 and older, is particularly important to women, who tend to live longer than men and have considerably less private retirement income. The average older woman spends significantly more of her annual income on health care (22 percent) than the average older man (17 percent).[29] Recent changes encourage beneficiaries to leave fee-for-service providers to take advantage of slightly more generous benefits at HMOs, but experts fear that the shift will raise costs and undermine the traditional Medicare program on which women rely.[30]

Meanwhile, the health component of the fiscal welfare system is likely to grow. This might take the form of a refundable tax credit to low-income households that don't have access to employer-based coverage. One change, already implemented, offers tax breaks to middle- and upper-income people who can set up health savings accounts or pay premiums on high-deductible health insurance policies.[31] Health economists warn that the availability of the tax credit as an alternative means of securing health insurance will almost certainly lead some employers to drop coverage for their workers. This in turn will increase the ranks of the uninsured among low- and moderate-income workers, a group that includes many women. The tax credits would also encourage younger and healthier employees to leave employment-based plans, leading to an increase in the cost of coverage for older and sicker workers that remain in the pools.[32]

Losing Security: Social Security. In December 2004, the National Women's Law Center urged women to take action to protect one of their most valuable sources of financial security: "Women should fight to protect and strengthen Social Security—because we're all more secure when we're in this together. Social Security embodies the American value of coming together to help one another, especially in times of need. Taking money out of Social Security and putting it into private accounts would unravel this system of mutual support—and women and their families especially would be worse for it."[33]

Social Security is probably the most popular government program, providing a modicum of economic security for almost every citizen over 65. Women account for 60 percent of Social Security beneficiaries, and the payments they receive represent a significant share of their income: 90 percent for almost one-third of all elderly women,[34] and 90 percent for half of all elderly unmarried Latinas and African American women.[35] Without Social Security, the poverty rate among older women would be 53 percent instead of the current 15 percent.[36] And Social Security disability and survivors' benefits are particularly important to African American women and Latinas, who are twice as likely as Whites to collect them.[37]

In an attempt to sell the American public on privatizing Social Security, supporters claim that the system is in crisis. According to *New York Times* columnist Paul Krugman, "[T]he politics of privatization depend crucially on convincing the public that the system is in imminent danger of collapse, that we must destroy Social Security in order to save it."[38] Privatizers and others who want to cut Social Security benefits point out that because of demographic shifts, the relative number of workers paying into the system is slowly decreasing compared to the number of people receiving benefits. Darcy Ann Olsen of the Cato Institute argues that "virtually every woman would be better-off financially under a system of fully private, personal retirement accounts with earnings sharing."[39] But as a result of Social Security tax increases initiated during the Reagan administration, the Social Security Trust Fund holds a reservoir of funding built up over the years when the payroll tax exceeded the amount paid out in benefits. In fact, at the end of December 2004, the Social Security Trust Fund had about $1,687 billion reserved for future use.[40] According to official projections, the current system will be viable until at least 2041.

Nor would privatization ensure that Social Security could continue to maintain current levels of retirement income after 2041. The online Social Security Accurate Benefit Calculator was created by the Institute for Women's Policy Research (IWPR) and the Center for Economic and Policy Research (CEPR). It enables taxpayers to compare Social Security benefits under both the current system and a proposed privatization plan. The Calculator shows that a person who is 25 years old, earning $28,000 a year, and planning to retire at age 67 without taking any years off from work would receive nearly one-third less with the privatized plan than with the current system. (Individuals can use the calculator at www.iwpr.org to estimate their own losses under such a proposal.)

Changes to the current program might threaten women's financial security in other ways, as well. According to Alicia Munnell of the Carroll School of Management at Boston College, "The present Social Security system offers a range of protections—progressive benefits formulas, dependents' benefits, lifetime benefits, and inflation adjustment—that are of great importance to women and not duplicated by any of the proposals to privatize the system ... These are established rights, promised by law. Women should be very reluctant to give them up for an untried system that relies on individual investments for even part of their basic retirement income."[41]

On the other hand, according to the Congressional Budget Office, if Congress canceled the recent tax cuts just for the top 1 percent of households, the increase in revenues over the next 75 years would be larger than the entire projected Social Security shortfall during those same 75 years. Others have suggested that Congress retain the estate tax on a small number of large estates, instead of repealing it altogether as planned, and dedicate the revenues to the Trust Fund.[42] Still others have proposed increasing or removing the cap on the salary level on which payroll taxes are levied so that more money could be raised from those who earn higher salaries. The bottom line, again according to Paul Krugman, is that "Social Security is a government program that works, a demonstration that a modest amount of taxing and spending can make people's lives better and more secure."[43]

A PERSONAL STORY: A SECURE RETIREMENT IN INSECURE TIMES

Barbara Taft counts her blessings. Although her husband has Alzheimer's disease and now lives in a nursing home, Taft, a White, retired special education teacher from Eden Prairie, Minnesota, feels incredibly lucky that their retirement savings, combined with Social Security, allows them to feel secure in their old age. Many people she cares about, however, are not as fortunate. And she worries about them.

"My daughter-in-law's mother is living on Social Security. She has medical problems and lives in low-cost senior housing. For a while there she was trying to decide whether she should eat or take her medication." If it had not been for Social Security and family help, Taft says, her daughter-in-law's mother would have been in dire straits.

And Taft worries about the future. "I'm very anxious to protect Social Security for my three sons because they may need it in the future. I hope they'll all be in reasonable shape financially when they retire, but you just don't know. There could be illness, and disabilities come up as you get older. One son is out of a job, and if he were at retirement age right now, he'd be in trouble."

She remembers her aunt who was very upset when President Roosevelt made Social Security payments mandatory back in the 1930s. Half a lifetime later, her aunt saw things differently. "When she retired from her job as a teacher, she didn't have a private pension—only Social Security and a bit of money she had saved. And I remember her saying to me, 'If Roosevelt were here, I would have to apologize to him. I am so ashamed of myself.'"

Back then, Taft explains, Social Security meant that the poverty was not as extreme and people were able to keep their homes. As that generation started to age, the desire to avoid becoming a burden on their families was strong. "It was then," Taft says, "that the realization of Social Security really hit home."

The future, as Taft knows firsthand, is uncertain. As the volunteer co-chair for public policy for Minnesota's chapter of the American Association of University Women, she feels strongly that we need to have basic retirement income that is dependable and secure. And as someone who knows what it's like to care for a loved one who is ill— she took care of her husband for ten years before he moved to the nursing home—she knows that the care-givers need help, too. "Now that doesn't mean that the government just takes care of everything without people putting in effort," Taft continues, passion rising in her voice. "But for one circumstance or another, people can't take care of all their needs."

When Barbara Taft taught high school, she worked with students with physical or emotional problems. "These are people who have to be dependent and are unable to provide for themselves for steady retirement income. If our country is interested in considering the moral elements of helping our people who are in need, both during their working years and at retirement age, then they will see that the government, in one form or another, will provide a secure environment for everyone."

No Shelter from the Storm: Housing. More than 6 million women in the United States pay more than 50 percent of their income to house themselves and their children. Recent studies link stable and affordable shelter to the health and well-being of families and to success in educating and socializing children.[44]

Programs such as *public housing* and *Section 8 housing subsidies*—providing vouchers that cover a portion of the rent for private housing—have been quite effective in serving those low-income households able to access help, a significant proportion of which are headed by women. The Office of Management and Budget reported in 2003 that the voucher program posts "improved efficiencies and cost effectiveness in achieving program goals each year."[45] However, funding for housing has fallen over the years. For some families, this has meant facing homelessness. For others, it has meant higher rents and less money for other vital household needs. And White House projections, designed to keep spending flat through 2010, demand cuts after inflation of $3 billion in housing assistance.[46]

An analysis of the administration's 2006 Budget Proposals by the American Federation of State, County, and Municipal Employees notes that a proposed cut of 11.5 percent in the Department of Housing and Urban Development's budget includes $252 million from the public housing capital fund, a zeroing-out of program funding for revitalization of severely distressed public housing (the HOPE VI program), $18 million from housing for persons with disabilities, and more than $1 billion from community development programs.[47]

Hungry for More: Nutrition. About 21.3 million people received *Food Stamps* each month in 2003, a 12 percent increase over the previous year. More than half the recipient households contained children, and most of these were headed by a single parent.[48] In fact, children and working-age women constitute 79 percent of the 19 million aided by Food Stamps.[49] The administration's budget proposal for 2006 would cut off Food Stamps from about 300,000 people by making it harder for working families with children to receive aid.[50]

More than 8 million women and children are enrolled in the *Women with Infants and Children Supplemental Nutrition Program (WIC)*.[51] But in order to achieve the administration's goal of keeping spending flat through the decade, WIC would be cut by 9.6 percent, depriving some 740,000 mothers and children of a vital source of basic nutrition.[52]

Who's Minding the Store: Small Businesses. Proposed budget cuts threaten the income source for growing numbers of women who struggle to maintain small businesses. The proposal slashes the *Small Business Administration* budget from $3.3 billion to $636 million in 2006,[53] cutting support for the 9.1 million women and 800,000 African Americans who are small business owners. The proposal allots no resources to the micro-loan program, which encourages business ownership on a very small scale in order to move families out of poverty— businesses like the restaurant that Diane Holloway, an out-of-work chef and single mother in Silver City, New Mexico, started with micro-loan funding, which now employs 30 workers.[54]

Going for Broke: Income Support. The National Women's Law Center's analysis of recent census data shows that poverty for women and children has grown each year since 2000, with poverty rates for adult women at 12.7 percent in 2004, 37 percent higher than the poverty rate for adult men.[55] In 2003 and 2004, the poverty rates grew both for single-mother and married couple families with children. And families in the lowest fifth of the income distribution—disproportionately female-headed households—received a smaller share of the nation's income in 2003 than at any point during the 37 years for which data has been collected: just 3.4 percent of the aggregate, a share that remained unchanged in 2004.[56]

But at the same time, income support for the poor has fallen. Beginning in the mid-1990s, the number of families receiving *welfare* declined precipitously, prompted both by a strong economy and by highly restrictive assistance policies ushered in when time-limited, welfare-to-work assistance—Temporary Aid to Needy Families (TANF)—replaced traditional welfare—Aid to Families with Dependent Children. When the economy soured just four years later, many families, especially those headed by women, lost the marginal financial gains they had struggled to achieve. A recent report from the Urban Institute shows that in 2002, breadwinners in 58 percent of families that left welfare are not employed, up from 50 percent in 1999.[57]

Particular groups of single mothers and children face the greatest hardships: those with younger children or children with serious health problems, women with chronic health problems, women of color, and non-English-speaking women with limited education. Poor immigrant families were particularly hard hit by changes to the welfare system since many legal immigrants were excluded from TANF benefits. Despite paying taxes from the moment they arrive, the majority of legal immigrants do not have access to TANF or social programs such as Food Stamps or Medicaid until they have resided in the United States for five years. Even after five years, they remain ineligible for Supplemental Security Income (SSI).[58]

The 2006 budget proposed by the administration includes flat funding of TANF despite these increases in poverty and despite inflation. This means that cash assistance will cover even less of the basic necessities for those fewer and fewer families who still receive it at all.

Feeling the Pinch: Women in Public Sector Jobs. Tax-supported programs play a major role in the lives of women as workers as well as taxpayers and program beneficiaries. Public sector employment has been a route into the middle class for many White women and women and men of color, especially before legal remedies were in place to address discrimination. Today more women than men hold government jobs as well as jobs in nonprofit and for-profit organizations supported by public funding.[59]

The public sector employs nearly 20 percent of all women workers (compared with 13 percent of men). This includes 22 percent of African American women, 17.6 percent of White women, and 14 percent of Latinas. While women's work in the public sector, as in the private sector, tends to be paid less,[60] the public sector provides many good jobs for women, and especially for women without college degrees.[61]

Society depends on the public sector for considerable education and care-giving work. While women are just under half of the workforce, they are 71 percent of the 6.2 million teachers in the United States, most of whom teach in public schools. They are 92 percent of registered nurses, 76 percent of all those employed in hospitals, 79 percent of those employed in other health services, and 82 percent of those who work in social services.[62] Although women now work as firefighters, bus drivers, and police officers, they remain the minority in these traditionally male occupations. But women continue to predominate as librarians, home health aides, and child-care workers, to name only a few of many sex-segregated occupations. Women are also overrepresented as public sector clerical and administrative support staff.

Mounting tax cuts and reduced government spending pose a serious threat to these women workers. As tax cuts limit the dollars available to pay for programs, jobs also disappear. And privatization of services over the last 25 years has led public sector employment to fall as a percentage of the overall workforce. The transfer of service jobs from the public to the private sector means lower pay, less union protection, and fewer health and retirement benefits for women. Given that programs providing care have been among the most heavily cut, all families and communities lose these needed supports.

A PERSONAL STORY: THE IMPORTANCE OF A HELPING HAND

Shirley Williams-Johnson remembers the day she got her first paycheck as if it was yesterday. She started work September 17, 1991, and received her first paycheck for half a pay period just a week later. "I can remember me and my kids jumping around, we were so happy."

Williams-Johnson, an African American woman, is the full-time manager of the Food Program at St. Paul's Women's Advocates Inc., the first shelter for battered women and their children in the United States. In 1989, she fled Milwaukee, Wisconsin, with her three youngest children to escape her physically abusive husband. She arrived at a shelter in Minnesota for a fresh and, most importantly, a safe start. After being homeless in California, Texas, and Wisconsin, Williams-Johnson was relieved when she found the assistance she so desperately needed in Minnesota.

Williams-Johnson was greeted in Minnesota by a wealth of resources both privately and publicly funded. In addition to MPHIP, Minnesota's version of Aid to Families with Dependent Children, she received Section 8 housing and Food Stamps for her family and earned a GED high school equivalency for herself. A community program, "Putting it All Together," helped her identify her skills and develop a resume, provided child-care and furniture vouchers, coached and clothed her for job interviews, and supplied bus fare to go on interviews.

Just months after leaving the shelter, Williams-Johnson started volunteering at various shelters across the Twin Cities and received training to be a relief advocate worker. Ultimately she was offered jobs at three different shelters.

Today Shirley Williams-Johnson lives in her own home with her second husband of ten years—and continues to give back to the community that provided her family with a fresh start. Her oldest son, who stayed behind in Milwaukee when she and her three other kids moved to Minnesota, has had the hardest time, but now he is settled with his own family and job. The others are in good places too, with college educations, families, and jobs; her daughter just graduated and married in June 2005. But Williams-Johnson says she is most proud that they are "all living free from abuse and free from being abusers! It's almost more than I could ask for."

Shirley Williams-Johnson was fortunate to have critical public resources available, as well as a strong spirit, to help her family get back on its feet. Today she would have a harder time accessing such resources. Changes in welfare policy and fiscally strapped states have led to reductions in human services, and many who are in need are turned away or on long waiting lists for housing and other public assistance. Moreover, public employees and other human service workers whose agencies depend on tax dollars, women and men like Williams-Johnson, fear for their jobs as agency budgets shrink. But for now she has work that pays her bills and fills her heart with a sense she is helping others.

WHAT THIS MEANS FOR WOMEN

Women—as consumers of public services and as public service workers—have a special stake in the viability of government programs. But current tax and spending policies are draining the U.S. Treasury, undermining the very programs women rely on.

Continuing on this course—and particularly, making permanent the 2001 and 2003 tax cuts—will have lasting effects on women through all stages of their lives: young women whose careers and family life are just beginning, women in midlife who receive tax credits for child-care and whose children enjoy public schools, and older women whose healthcare costs continue to spiral out of control.

As vital publicly funded services are squeezed, women's choices are increasingly limited. For many women and their families, cuts to these services have already diminished their quality of life. And without changes in tax and spending policies, the future only promises more bad news for more women. In the short term, vital public services will shrink even further as the huge tax cuts, together with expanded military spending, continue to create enormous deficits. And in the long term, the growing national debt will burden the next generations of women (and men).

Because the effect of the tax system is so broad, and so lasting, it has enormous potential to affect women's lives—for better or for worse.

STRAIGHT TALK ABOUT WOMEN AND TAXES: HOW TO MAKE THE CASE

To those who say: There is so much waste and bureaucracy that we should be able to provide the same services with less money—and besides, we don't need all these government programs. Let's just cut taxes.

We say: The tax cuts are like a late-night infomercial that promises to "put more money in your pocket and it won't cost you a thing." You can't believe the hype. In fact, these tax cuts cost us enormously—and are especially damaging to women.

- Already seriously underfunded programs—for Head Start, education, fire and police protection, and health services, for example—are in jeopardy.
- Most Americans want such programs maintained: asked whether they prefer a tax cut or increased domestic spending on education and health programs, better than two-thirds of Americans favor increased spending.
- Social Security was put in place to address real social and financial emergencies—and it worked. We no longer have large numbers of the elderly living in grinding poverty. Proposals to privatize the system don't address its financial needs, but do diminish the "security" in Social Security. Ask the Enron employees whose pensions were invested in company stock how they feel about private accounts.

- When domestic programs are starved for funds, women suffer at all stages of their lives—as college students depending on Pell Grants, as mothers responsible for the care and education of their children, as older women relying on Medicare and Social Security for their basic needs.

REAL WOMEN NEED REAL TAX REFORM: A CALL TO ACTION

The progressive community must come together around tax and budget issues in a way that they have never done before. We need to get out of defense—fighting tax cuts all the time—and turn to the kinds of proactive, long-term strategies that promote a progressive tax system, a fair tax system that raises sufficient revenue to advance our priorities—to help ourselves, our families, our country, to bring back some of the values of community that are the basis of a progressive tax system.

—Joan Entmacher, Vice President of Family Economic Security, National Women's Law Center

Behind the huge numbers, the wealth of statistics, and the seemingly dry and impenetrable topic of taxes is the real need to understand and change the tax system. Throughout this book, we've threaded stories about women taxpayers, women public sector workers, and women who rely on key publicly funded programs. Real tax reform would benefit all these women, but not only them. The tax story told in this book underscores the importance of a fair and adequate tax system for everyone—and the challenges we face in shaping *real* tax policy reform.

As long as we depend on basic public services, we all need a tax system that provides sufficient resources for the parts of our government that promote broad economic security, a healthy and educated populace, environmental and public safety, equitable opportunity, and essential support for the very young, the very old, and those otherwise in need.

As long as women earn less than men, have greater responsibilities for care-giving across generations, and have less wealth, they need a tax system that is progressive to the core, that taxes wealth at a rate at least as high as work, and that generates the revenues necessary to support vital social programs and services.

As long as women and men of color face discrimination and live with legacies of economic and social disadvantages, they too need a tax system that is fair, one that is free of gender and racial bias and that supports those seeking to join or to stay in the middle class.

As long as our economy produces so many low-wage jobs, families dependent on those jobs need tax policies that promote access to high-quality public education, human services, housing, health care, and retirement security among many other important government services. And all of us need policies that encourage a strong economy that can ultimately provide good jobs with living wages to all our residents.

As long as the gap between the wealthy and the poor is as stark as it is today, we all benefit from progressive tax policies that help close that gap, so that the economic and political conditions that are the foundation of security and democracy can be sustained.

This book is a call for new tax policies that assure adequate resources and that more equitably distribute the responsibility for paying for the government services we all need and use. In defining taxes as a woman's issue, we argue that fair and equitable tax policies are central to the larger goal of promoting equality, opportunity, and social justice for all women, indeed, for all *people*.

Advocates for women have long fought for workplace equity; for civil, human, and reproductive rights; for freedom from violence and abuse; and for other issues popularly recognized as "women's issues." But as we have shown in this book, taxes are also a woman's issue. While women's needs and interests vary widely, especially by race and class, as a group they experience tax policies in specific ways. Tax policies that disadvantage women, that promote economic polarization, and that fail to generate the revenues necessary to support essential programs for all endanger the well-being of individual women and children, threaten the stability of our families and communities, and undermine our nation's ability to compete globally

We believe that a fair and just tax system depends on an honest, transparent, and well-informed debate about tax policy. Women must be prepared to participate in this debate—as taxpayers, consumers of government services, paid and unpaid workers, public sector employees, and decision-makers in a democracy. By insisting upon fairness and accountability from government officials and legislators, women can weigh various tax proposals —perhaps skeptically, but not cynically—in light of their own experiences and solid facts. As Noleen Heyzer, executive director of UNIFEM, stated in 2005, "Each one of us can ask questions about what happens to our taxes, and what happens to the money that we give to our government. Because you use your life to create your wealth, and you are giving part of your wealth to the government, you need to make sure that it's used for the common good. The government budget, at the end of the day, is your budget."[1]

WHAT WOULD REAL TAX REFORM LOOK LIKE?

The tax system did not become unfair, inadequate, inequitable, or complex overnight, under one presidential administration or because of one political party. And reforming the system won't be easy or simple, either. There's no quick fix or single answer. But five principles—based on new questions and straight answers—can help women reframe the debate about taxes, tax policy, and the national budget:

1. Fairness. Who will benefit the most and who the least from various changes to tax policies? What is the impact on the after-tax income of various women and their families? Is the system based on ability to pay? Will the changes mean that it will be very difficult for lower-income families to afford their basic needs after paying taxes? Will those who have the most disposable income and who benefit the most from our current economic and social arrangements pay their fair share?

2. Equity. Do taxpayers with similar incomes and similar needs pay similar levels of taxes and receive similar benefits from the system? Does the system contain gender or racial biases? Does a particular policy harm women and other workers whose wages are taxed heavily through income and payroll taxes, while at the same time offering large breaks to those who earn substantial income through investments? Are needs served by the nation's social welfare system treated equitably, as compared with the benefits enjoyed by those who can take advantage of the tax breaks available through the fiscal welfare system?

3. Adequacy. Does overall tax policy provide the revenues necessary for a reasonable level of the public services so important to all, and especially to women and their families? Does it ensure adequate funds for the services the government should provide, including a safety net that protects the old, the young, those who are ill or disabled, the poor, and anyone else who falls on hard times?

4. Responsibility. Do policies at the federal level simply shift the weight of public services to overburdened state and local systems—systems that generally secure funding through more regressive taxes? Do they shift more of the burden of care to women? Do tax policies shift the cost of current expenditures to future generations by borrowing excessively? Are the terms of this "mortgage" transparent, or are they hidden in today's budget so that they will balloon in years to come?

5. National goals. Does a particular tax policy enhance the quality of life for all women—in fact, for all Americans—regardless of their race, age, ethnicity, sexual orientation, marital status, or class? Does it widen the already large gap between the wealthy and middle- and lower-income earners? Does it allow all women and their families to have a basic level of economic security? Does it support and maintain a vigorous middle class? Will it mean that corporations pay their fair share of taxes while at the same time encouraging them to stay in local communities? Does it encourage investment in our nation's future, including a healthy and educated new generation of Americans? Will it ensure that the United States can remain competitive in the global marketplace? Does it provide for our national security, in all the meanings of that term?

WHAT POLICY CHANGES WOULD PROMOTE REAL TAX REFORM?

As everyone knows, the federal tax code is a maze of rules and regulations—54,846 pages worth, to be exact.[2] But tax simplification is not a substitute for tax fairness or for ensuring that the government has sufficient revenues to meet the basic needs of the country. Nor does everyone need to plow through all 54,846 pages or understand each tax provision in order to become effective advocates for fair tax policy.

What we do need is a robust debate about how to structure federal, state, and local tax systems. In a fair system, women would not lose out, racial disparities would be corrected, taxes would be based on ability to pay, low- and moderate-income taxpayers would have enough after-tax income to care for their families, and we all would share the responsibility for creating a safe, just, and economically sound nation.

What are some of the changes that would help us achieve that tax system—and how can we help bring about those changes? First, there are some actions we can take in the short term.

- Collect and make available gender and racially disaggregated data, so that we can better evaluate how tax policies affect different groups in our society.
- Reject efforts to make permanent the 2001 and 2003 tax cuts on capital gains, dividends, and high incomes. In fact, support their roll-back to help provide sufficient tax revenue for current needs, reduce the deficit, and promote effective progressive taxation.
- Maintain the estate tax for those who are the wealthiest among us. This will increase revenue and discourage the untenable concentration of wealth at the very top of the income scale that has been growing in recent decades.
- Protect tax breaks like the Earned Income Tax Credit and the Child Tax Credit that help those who most need the added after-tax income. Extend the benefits of such breaks to those whose incomes are so low that they don't currently qualify.
- Address the growing impact of the Alternative Minimum Tax on middle-income earners and ensure that it applies only to the high-income earners it was designed to affect. This will make the tax system more progressive.

- Oppose efforts to privatize or reduce Social Security, a policy change that would seriously undermine the nation's ability to ensure a minimal level of economic security for older Americans, as well as for those who are disabled and the families of deceased workers.
- Challenge current and future budget proposals that cut funding for education, health care, human services, public safety, and other critical tax-supported programs. Sustaining these programs is essential if we want to support women's care work in the home and ensure a fair, adequate, productive, and globally competitive society.
- Ensure that businesses pay their fair share of taxes and structure them to create positive incentives for businesses to treat employees fairly—that is, to supply health and other vital employer-provided benefits—and to contribute to environmental sustainability and worker safety. Repeal tax code provisions that reward them for outsourcing jobs, despoiling the environment, undermining the health and welfare of communities, and sheltering money on which they should pay their fair share of taxes.

Other reforms may require a longer-term approach:
- Promote a more progressive overall tax system—at the federal, but also the state and local levels—that asks people to give in relationship to their ability to pay.
- Promote the development of a universal system of public benefits that serves all Americans across the economic spectrum. Funded by progressive taxes and building on the popularity of Social Security, these benefits would assist in meeting everyone's need for an adequate level of income, health, education, shelter, employment, and social services. These benefits would pay special attention to the social and economic security of those with the fewest resources. Such a system of care would address both basic human needs and meet broad national goals.
- Prioritize reforms that sustain, rather than eliminate or privatize, programs that help individuals and families whatever their economic status, such as Social Security, Medicare, and Unemployment Insurance. Ensure that reforms focused on the fiscal viability of these programs adhere to the principle of progressivity in generating program revenues. Avoid pri-

vatization, which often means the end of access to services and programs for the most disadvantaged, and greater insecurity for the rest of us.

- Ensure greater transparency of the tax code to make it easy to negotiate and clear in terms of who benefits and who loses from changes to the system. But do not trade tax simplification for tax fairness. We can have both!

- Promote tax and economic literacy for all. That is, enhance public understanding of government functions, and the relationship between tax collections, government spending, and the quality of life. Encourage broader public dialogue and participation—especially of women—in setting fiscal and social policies.

CALL TO ACTION

Of course, we need to do more than educate ourselves, more than talk to our neighbors and friends. We need to act. Fortunately, we do not have to take on these reforms alone, simply as individuals. We know the power of organization, cooperation, and advocacy in creating positive change—as well as in preventing the implementation of policies that harm the social and economic fabric of our nation. The evolution of the Earned Income Tax Credit into one vital tool to address poverty, the implementation of family and medical leave policies at the national and local levels, even the slow-down in the momentum toward privatization of Social Security, all attest to the hard and effective work of individuals and organizations, many of them in the Council's network, to ensure that our nation's policies address the needs of all our people. Our successes—and the challenges that remain—underscore the need for more work that looks across economic class, race, and gender borders; for more cross-sector coalitions that bring activists, scholars, advocates, and policymakers together; and for more efforts to broaden public debates and build inclusive communities to address the challenges that confront us.

So as the nation works its way through this contentious and complicated debate on tax policy and public spending, we must join together with those who are already taking action for a more progressive tax system. In this volume, we have gathered ideas from some of those scholars and advocates in the network of the National Council for Research on Women who are working on issues related to taxation. Their insights reflect multiple approaches, providing food for thought and action. We have also included a resource guide that lists some of the key research centers, think tanks, advocacy organizations, and other groups that work on tax issues or on economic and social policy focused on women. Along with the work of these important groups, the cause of promoting a more just tax system will need the attention, the commitment, and the hard work of all of us.

We may not all agree about every aspect of real tax reform, and not all reforms will affect us in the same way or to the same degree. But despite the many differences among women, it is clearly possible to create a system of taxes and social policies based on the principles of progressivity, fairness, adequacy, responsibility, and equity—a system that creates a solid foundation for strong families and communities, robust and sustainable businesses, innovative institutions and enterprises, and real democracy. Our hope is that a more tax-literate, activist movement of women can contribute to these ends on behalf of themselves and the future of this country.

FORUM: VIEWS FROM THE COUNCIL'S NETWORK OF CENTERS

This volume, with its broad overview of women and taxes, is built on the work of many experts from the National Council for Research on Women. Many of them have conducted research, undertaken analysis, and reframed issues in reaction to specific policy proposals or around specific aspects of women's work and the need to advocate for women and their families in specific circumstances. Based on their research and analysis, many have introduced innovative policy recommendations. Seldom have they had the opportunity to share their ideas and examine them in the context of an overall understanding of how tax and spending policies affect women.

In developing this book, the authors heard from many of these experts. Council scholars and researchers approached the subject of women and taxes from diverse angles, from the relationship between tax policy and services like child-care or higher education to the ways taxes impact young women to how women's unpaid care work is recognized within the tax system. They looked at ways in which policymakers can support women and their families by addressing the issue on the state and local level, or by expanding tax credits and other policies that support families. Some saw U.S. tax policy in an international context, others through the specific experiences of people of color, and still others from the point of view of recent tax cuts and policy changes. And others helped us reframe taxation by asking us to think in alternative ways—for example, to look at some taxes as insurance, or to consider alternative tax structures that can provide added revenue and reward employers with women-friendly policies.

These experts were not always in agreement, even on some issues central to women's experience of the tax system. For example, several of them point out the possible conflict between our goal of recognizing the unpaid care work that women undertake in the home and of ensuring that women who work for pay outside the home are not penalized. To understand and resolve these differences, economists, policymakers, and scholars must come together to develop a more comprehensive framework for understanding and resolving these conflicts—a framework that must include women's unique experiences and perspectives.

But all of these experts shared a fundamental understanding of the absolutely essential role of government, and therefore taxes, in the lives of women, girls, and their families and communities. Sandra Morgen, an author of this book and director of the Center for the Study of Women and Society at the University of Oregon, identifies that role in the first piece in this chapter—her call for a greater understanding of the fundamental relationship between a fair tax system and one that generates sufficient revenues for the programs we need.

The short pieces that follow express some of the thoughts and recommendations of experts from Council member centers, captured in their specific voices and framed from the perspectives of their individual work.

A FAIR TAX SYSTEM: THE CHALLENGE

SANDRA MORGEN, DIRECTOR, CENTER FOR THE STUDY OF WOMEN IN SOCIETY, UNIVERSITY OF OREGON

Tax policy in this country has long been hotly contested at both the national and state levels. Since the late 1970s, conservative policymakers have garnered the support of a growing number of middle- and low-income constituents with promises to cut, or at least not to raise, taxes. Yet a large proportion of voters tell pollsters and researchers that they value public policies and programs that ensure access to education, health care, retirement security, and help for the poor. Such support remains solid even when they are asked to weigh funding for these programs against tax cuts. And Americans, by and large, support the principle of a progressive tax system.

It is important to use research to better understand what can be seen as a contradiction between supporting programs and opposing the revenues necessary to fund these programs—and, using solid data, to help the general public understand that there is no necessary conflict between a fair tax system and one that generates sufficient revenues for these important programs.

Over the past decade, the CSWS Welfare research team has documented countless ways in which low-income families are negatively affected when programs that subsidize otherwise unaffordable health care, child care, housing, and other basic needs are cut in the name of privatization or "personal responsibility," or because elected officials tell us that we cannot "afford" such programs. This volume has amply demonstrated that women, communities of color, and the poor have already lost a great deal, and stand to lose much more, in the wake of enormous tax cuts and policies that have shifted the proportional burden of taxes downward onto middle- and low-income families. So what can we do?

As researchers, we can use our skills and resources to document the differential impact of tax cuts by gender, race, and class, and the relationship between tax policy and economic security across race, class, and gender.

As teachers, we can bring information about taxes, including the history of tax policy and contemporary debates about taxes, into our classrooms as we strive to promote greater economic literacy, and particularly tax literacy, among our students.

As advocates, we can support reforms that promote a more progressive tax policy at the national, state, and local levels; refundable credits targeting low-income families; and budget policies that help promote economic security for those currently disadvantaged by tax and spending policies.

As voters, we can demand that our elected representatives be accountable for real tax reform that reverses the 25-year trend toward favoring the wealthy and corporations at the expense of the rest of us.

A FAIR TAX SYSTEM: NECESSARY CHANGES

NANCY FOLBRE, PROFESSOR OF ECONOMICS, UNIVERSITY OF MASSACHUSETTS, AMHERST; MEMBER, INTERNATIONAL ASSOCIATION FOR FEMINIST ECONOMICS

What we need to do in the short run:

Tax those most able to pay by:

- ending the phase-out of the estate tax;
- eliminating the cap on taxable Social Security income;
- eliminating the mortgage interest deduction for second and third homes; and
- improving enforcement efforts to reduce cheating.

Help those with low incomes and support care-giving by:

- increasing the child-care deduction and making it fully refundable for households with incomes of $50,000 or less, with a phase-out for more affluent families;
- reducing the phase-out of the Earned Income Tax Credit so more families can benefit and providing increased benefits for larger families (they now do not increase beyond two children);
- increasing the Child Tax Credit and making it fully refundable; and
- providing up to five years' worth of care-giver credits for Social Security to individuals who take time out of paid employment to care for children or other family members.

What we need to do in the long run:

Simplify the tax system and provide tools for people to better understand what they have paid in and what they have gotten, or can expect to get, out.

Tax the rich and the wasteful: more progressive income taxes could ease the burden of increased sales taxes on oil and other forms of carbon consumption.

Tax individuals, not families: eliminate both marriage penalties and bonuses. Assign exemptions and credits for children on the basis of who actually cares for them.

A FAIR TAX SYSTEM: ADVANCING WOMEN'S PRIORITIES—AND THOSE OF THE NATION

KATHY ROGERS, PRESIDENT, LEGAL MOMENTUM

Taxes involve two sets of issues. The first is what we collect from whom. The second is how we invest what we collect, and who benefits. Women are a growing number of taxpayers and they rely more heavily on government-funded programs, such as Medicare and Social Security. So on both counts women must be an influential part of the public debate on tax and spending policies.

What are women's priorities? Certainly nothing as simplistic as "smaller government" or "no new taxes." In our democracy the government exists to do what the people want it to do. It's not an independent adversary that has to be cut down to size. The question isn't, "What's the right size of government?" The question is, "What's the government's effectiveness in providing what matters most to women?"

These priorities include national security and a healthy economy. Too often overlooked, however, is the fact that they also include healthy communities and healthy families. For women, social responsibility and individual responsibility are not mutually exclusive, but mutually supportive.

So while the current debate focuses on how to reduce taxes, we should insist upon a debate on where to invest our taxes in order to advance women's priorities. If it's a good investment, we'll pay the taxes necessary. For example, one women's priority that is barely on the radar screen of policymakers is quality, affordable child-care for every family that wants it. Early care and education is ignored or dismissed with the argument that it is too expensive. In fact, it is a very wise investment of our taxes. Clearly, we know that quality care is good for children and helps parents carry out their responsibilities and take the best care they can of their families. That should be return enough. But it is also a good financial investment.

We also know from recent research that the return on investment of quality early care and education is superior to many economic development programs paid for with public dollars. In many states, the early care and education industry is large enough to rival other major economic sectors, such as the pharmaceutical and hotel/hospitality industries. Every dollar invested in quality early care and education saves the taxpayer as much as $13 in future costs (in areas such as foster care, criminal justice, remedial education, and welfare).[1]

PERSPECTIVES: A GIRL-FRIENDLY TAX POLICY
HEATHER JOHNSTON NICHOLSON, DIRECTOR OF RESEARCH, GIRLS INCORPORATED

In an survey conducted in 2000 by Girls Inc. and Harris Interactive Survey, one twelfth-grade girl said, "We're expected to be beautiful, thin, intelligent, perfect women and manage everything else in our lives. I work thirty hours a week, keep up my grades, do college work, pay the bills and try to find time for sleep, maybe four to five hours a night."[2]

The stress most women experience as they manage paid work and unpaid care work is evident also in the lives of girls. Many girls have three jobs in the family economy: they work for low wages outside the home, bring homework from school so they'll be employable in the future, and do "home work"—cook, clean, and care for their siblings while the adults in the family work for pay. In too many families, this means girls are giving up after-school enrichments vital to their own personal and career development.

So in a society that reduces taxes for the wealthiest 1 percent while cutting support for public education, child-care, after-school, and youth development programs, most girls lose ground. When funds for TANF, Head Start, Title X (the provision of the Federal Public Health Service Act focused on family planning information and sources), Medicaid, and nutrition programs are cut, girls in the poorest families suffer.

It is up to us as individuals and as a society to see that every girl (and boy) has encouragement and support to stay—as we say at Girls Inc.— strong, smart, and bold. What follows is a list of some of the changes we would need to make to create a girl-friendly tax policy.

- Lower payroll taxes, or set them to begin above minimum wage rates.
- Exempt sales tax on food, clothing, and health-care items.
- Tax alcohol and tobacco to invest in youth development and prevention strategies.

- Continue and expand the State Children's Health Insurance Program (SCHIP).
- Extend TANF eligibility to students and to pregnant and parenting teens, whether or not they are living in their parents' homes.
- Expand meal programs at schools and community organizations.
- Invest in safe, supportive alternatives for young people who cannot live at home.
- Use investment of resources rather than testing as the primary means to ensure quality education for every young person.
- Put recess, physical education, the arts, comprehensive sexuality education, hands-on science and technology, and after-school program opportunities back into every school.
- Find out who is not finishing high school and who is not going on to higher education, and create new strategies and policies for full inclusion.

PERSPECTIVES: A STUDENT-FRIENDLY TAX POLICY

LUCIE LAPOVSKY, PROFESSOR OF ECONOMICS AND FORMER PRESIDENT, MERCY COLLEGE

Today, more than 53 percent of the students in our colleges and universities are women. But for those students with lower incomes, financing their education has become more and more difficult.

The major sources of government support are direct funding of public colleges by state and local governments and federal Pell Grants for low-income students. State and local support has increased by 10.7 percent during the last five years, but tuition has increased by 46 percent at public four-year colleges and by 26 percent at public two-year colleges as institutions scramble to keep up with higher costs. During the same period, the maximum Pell Grant ($4,050 today) has increased only 14.5 percent. Taking a longer view, the value of the Pell Grant has decreased since 1979 (when it was worth $4,548 in today's dollars), while tuition and fees, measured in constant dollars, have increased more than 150 percent in the same period.[3]

For families able to save money, the federal government has increased support for higher education through tax benefits, specifically higher education IRAs and 529 plans. And two new tax credits—the Hope credit and the

Lifetime Learning credit—help some students and their families finance their educations. Neither, however, is of value to those who do not owe taxes, making them regressive on the low end, nor to those with high incomes since they are phased out at higher levels of income.

PERSPECTIVES: THE CHALLENGE TO WOMEN OF COLOR

BONNIE THORNTON DILL, DIRECTOR, CONSORTIUM ON RACE, GENDER AND ETHNICITY AND PROFESSOR AND CHAIR, DEPARTMENT OF WOMEN'S STUDIES, UNIVERSITY OF MARYLAND, COLLEGE PARK

It is urgent that Black women and men and other people of color learn about and become actively engaged in this discussion of tax policy. Our work at the Consortium on Race, Gender, and Ethnicity, along with so much other research and writing, demonstrates how poor people, especially Black, Latina, and Native American Indian women, suffer the health and educational disadvantages of poverty, but are demonized by our society for using benefits that will improve their lives and the lives of their children.

As this book explains, current tax policy creates even greater divisions between the haves and have-nots because it routinely benefits wealthy citizens and increases the tax bill for the middle class. It helps explain why people who believe in equity and in eliminating racial, ethnic, and gender disparities find themselves believing they must abandon those values in order to sustain their family's well-being. The pressure on the middle class is compounded by recent changes to the tax system, which are helping drain the U.S. Treasury, enlarge the federal budget deficit, and raise the national debt. Women and men of color, a disproportionate number of whom are poor, and other poor people will be hurt first and suffer longest, but their plight is merely the vanguard for the rest of the middle class.

Black Americans, who have been in the forefront of social changes that have benefited so many other U.S. citizens throughout history, must include tax policy as an important arena for social change because a truly progressive tax system can help the poor and benefit working women, men, and children throughout society.

PERSPECTIVES: WOMEN FACING RETIREMENT

M. CINDY HOUNSELL, EXECUTIVE DIRECTOR, WOMEN'S INSTITUTE FOR A SECURE RETIREMENT (WISER)

Success in achieving economic equality for women and families will depend on new strategies and focus among women's organizations to affect tax policy. In general, many Americans do not understand how the tax system affects their quality of life, and many of our policymakers do not understand how some Americans live. The effects of Hurricane Katrina have called attention to the fact that many people in our country do not have access to economic opportunities that policymakers take for granted.

The shift away from traditional pensions has meant that many workers are on their own for retirement. Fewer than one out of five workers now has access to a funded pension plan with guaranteed benefits, and less than half of the workforce has any type of retirement plan. We are concerned about the retirement future of baby boomer women as more cuts loom for the programs like Social Security and Medicare, which older women count on. And we are concerned because of the way the current private retirement system works: that is, creating what may be a false sense of security by promoting investment in employer retirement plans, which in turn permit pretax investment and tax-deferred growth. The typical retirement savings plan account, for example, a 401(k) account, has about $55,000 in the account balance—an amount that will last for only a few years of retirement. They are not an adequate or reliable replacement for old-style pensions, which they have in many cases replaced.

Yet, policymakers try to solve these problems by provisions such as increasing the allowable annual contribution amounts in individual retirement accounts (IRAs) from $2,000 to $4,000. Since only an estimated 7 percent of eligible American workers contribute to such IRAs at the lower amount of $2,000, one might ask whether increasing the limit to $4,000 would persuade more people to contribute. For average- and lower-income workers, funding one's retirement plan is clearly not a priority—or a realistic possibility. As wages are eroded, there are usually more immediate needs.

There was, however, one retirement provision in the 2001 tax legislation that helped people of low to moderate means: the Savers Tax Credit. This provision will sunset in 2006, and we need to work together to expand it and keep it. Basically, it provides an extra incentive for eligible workers to save for retirement by providing a nonrefundable credit for making a salary deferral to an employer-sponsored retirement plan or to an IRA. We need to provide a great deal of education to workers to help them seize such opportunities when possible, and we need to broaden such policies to make the tax system a little fairer.

TAXES ON THE STATE AND LOCAL LEVEL: RESTORING THE PROMISE

TIM MCFEELEY, EXECUTIVE DIRECTOR AND BERNIE HORN, POLICY DIRECTOR AND EDITOR OF *RESTORING THE PROMISE OF AMERICA*, CENTER FOR POLICY ALTERNATIVES

With the White House and Congress dominated by those intent on cutting taxes, cutting government revenues, and moving more of the tax bill from the very wealthy to middle- and low-income wage earners, progressives need to focus on tax and spending policies at the state and local levels. For example, state legislators can implement policies to:

- create a more graduated income tax;
- close loopholes like credits and deductions;
- decouple the state estate tax from the federal one and continue to tax estates if Congress allows the phase-out at the federal level; and
- reform corporate taxation to ensure that corporations pay their fair share.

Such policies will help ensure that the costs for public services are shared in a way that doesn't hurt those at the bottom and middle of the income scale, while still providing enough income to fund services at the state level for women and their families.

(For specific recommendations for your state, please see the 2005 Progressive Agenda for the States, *Restoring the Promise of America*, at www.cfpa.org.)

TAXES ON THE STATE AND LOCAL LEVEL: CONFRONTING POVERTY

RONNIE STEINBERG, EXECUTIVE DIRECTOR, WOMEN'S SOCIAL POLICY AND RESEARCH CENTER, VANDERBILT UNIVERSITY

Our research shows that instituting progressive state income taxes can significantly reduce the disproportionate sales tax bill women pay at the state level. In addition, refundable state Earned Income Tax Credits can help further relieve the tax bill for women at the state level. State EITCs support work, as earnings are required for eligibility. They also reduce poverty, particularly if they are refundable, by decreasing the tax burden on low-income families and by supplementing income.

REFRAMING TAXATION: TAXES AS SOCIAL INSURANCE

EILEEN APPELBAUM, DIRECTOR, CENTER FOR WOMEN AND WORK, RUTGERS UNIVERSITY

Some taxes we pay—like Social Security and Unemployment Insurance taxes—are more like insurance. We all want the security they provide for individuals when they are unable to work. Because we all share the cost of these insurance policies, they are very economical.

We should expand this framework to cover paid family leave so that care-givers, most often women, can forgo their paychecks for a period of time to care for newborns, for the critically ill, or to attend to other family emergencies. It is not the kind of benefit we can ask employers to cover single-handedly. But it is something we can address as a society by instituting a shared payroll "insurance premium," like our current Unemployment Insurance tax.

Look at California—they've done it.

California's program, enacted in 2002, went into effect in July 2004. It supplements the federal Family and Medical Leave Act, which allows for twelve weeks of unpaid leave, by enabling most California workers to receive 55 percent of their salary for up to six weeks a year when they take family leave. The program is financed by payroll contributions. A number of states are closely observing the California model and may replicate the program.

REFRAMING TAXATION: TAXES FOR PROGRESSIVE CHANGE

GALE SUMMERFIELD, DIRECTOR, WOMEN AND GENDER IN GLOBAL PERSPECTIVES PROGRAM, UNIVERSITY OF ILLINOIS, URBANA-CHAMPAIGN

In general, we need to protect Social Security insurance and retirement benefits. The government is in a much better position to weather fluctuations in the economy than individuals relying on personal accounts.

We must design tax policy to provide adequate health care for all residents. Denying care to those temporarily unemployed, to those who have family members with high-cost illnesses who cannot get new coverage, to recent immigrants, or to anyone living in our midst hurts us all.

Tax reforms must reduce discrimination against women who work and avoid long-term incentives to keep women out of the labor force. Now, as economist Barbara Bergmann has pointed out, a woman who has worked outside the home can receive lower retirement benefits from her social security account than a woman with the same family income who worked only as an unpaid homemaker.

U.S. tax policy can be designed to help women globally. Development economist Ruth Pearson has proposed a "Maria Tax," where a portion of tax proceeds from international transactions would go to improve gender equity, child care, health care, and so on. We could increase the percentage of government revenue that goes directly to poor countries as aid, making sure that payments go to women as well as men. And poor countries that train health-care workers only to have them relocate to rich countries for better paying jobs could be compensated.

Like James Tobin's "Tobin Tax," which proposes a tax on cross-border currency trades, the Maria Tax reflects a global view of the economy and is based on an understanding of how profits are now generated through international trade. The Maria Tax would tax the value of foreign currency exchange in certain international transactions and provide funding to promote gender equality and compensate for the lack of protections and benefits that women often experience, especially in developing countries. Only a concept at this stage, the tax could be levied in proportion to the number of women in the labor force of the producer, and be paid by the importer in order not to penalize those who hire women. If the tax were applied globally, some of the incentives for companies to move abroad would be undermined.[4]

REFRAMING TAXATION: THE GLOBAL VIEWPOINT

KATHLEEN BARNETT, VICE PRESIDENT AND CAREN GROWN, DIRECTOR OF POVERTY REDUCTION AND ECONOMIC GOVERNANCE, INTERNATIONAL CENTER FOR RESEARCH ON WOMEN (ICRW)

In a major project undertaken in 2004 by the International Center for Research on Women for the Commonwealth Secretariat, researchers found that tax policy is critically important to gender equity in the developing world, for several reasons.

First, women in developing countries are predominantly poor, so it is essential that national tax structures give priority to principles of progressivity and ability to pay. Second, women—because of responsibilities for reproductive and subsistence work—are especially burdened by the lack of basic public infrastructure and services, and decisions about tax and other revenue policies that can support needed investment in these public goods have special importance for them. Third, the vast majority of women in developing countries are economically active, and the contributions of their labor—whether in kind or in cash—are crucial to their households, so tax policies that recognize women's productive efforts, including their ability to own economic resources such as land and to control their own sources of income, are especially important.

Finally, tax policy, in affecting the income, consumption, and investment decisions of individuals as well as businesses, shapes a country's path of social and economic development and the allocation of benefits that accrue from such development. In developing countries, where these outcomes are literally an issue of life and death for millions, it is especially important that women are part of the public policy debate. To participate in this debate, women in developing countries, and all public policymakers concerned with equitable development, need information on the impact of alternative tax policies.

Toward this end, international donors should support:

- national systems for collection and maintenance of sex-disaggregated data on income distribution and other economic variables;
- research on gender differences in economic roles and productivity, and on the impact of tax laws and policies by gender and by income class;

- mechanisms for dissemination and communication of information to the public; and
- structures for ensuring women's active participation in public policy decision making.

REFRAMING TAXATION: TOWARD A FEMINIST TAX POLICY
HEIDI HARTMANN, PRESIDENT, INSTITUTE FOR WOMEN'S POLICY RESEARCH

Feminists need to devote some time, effort, and political skill to working out model tax programs at all levels of government that would improve gender equity, accomplish other important goals, and gain widespread support from women and their representatives. Having adequate revenues to support necessary and desirable government programs is especially crucial to women, who typically rely on public services more than men do. Many women's groups, however, focus on specific program areas, such as domestic violence, breast cancer, abortion rights, job training, or education (to name just a few areas where women's groups are active), seeking to win legislative authorization and specific appropriation levels without explicitly considering the overall budget on either the tax or spending side.

Tax policy is the key to the size and nature of government. More of us need to get involved, hammer out our internal differences, and develop and push a coherent, feminist proposal for tax reform.

Developing a feminist tax program will be challenging. For example, while an idea like taxing individuals, not families, sounds appealing from a feminist perspective, doing so would likely also reduce the overall progressivity of the income tax system since it would allow some types of high-income families to be taxed at lower rates. For another example, improving benefits for working wives in Social Security sounds good, but it conflicts with improving benefits for women or men who are primarily family care-givers. Both objectives cost money, and they have differing effects on the goal of increasing gender equality, since one would encourage greater paid employment by women and the other might encourage women to spend more time care-giving. Reducing payroll taxes for lower-wage workers is appealing on the grounds of increasing progressivity, but if it contributed to the development of means testing for benefit receipt, it could lead to the eventual dismantling of Social Security. Tax policy typically meets some goals better than others, but to date feminist goals have rarely even been in the mix.

Despite the challenges, our need for a feminist framework with which to evaluate tax and budget policy is great. First and foremost, more feminists should be adding their voices to the debate.

APPENDIX A: GUIDE TO RESOURCES ON WOMEN AND TAXES

MEMBER CENTERS OF THE NATIONAL COUNCIL FOR RESEARCH ON WOMEN WORKING ON TAX ISSUES

The following member centers of the National Council for Research on Women have important information available on their websites, as well as in newsletters and e-updates, regarding tax and expenditure policies and economic security more broadly.

AMERICAN ASSOCIATION OF UNIVERSITY WOMEN (AAUW)

http://www.aauw.org

The AAUW's Public Policy and Government Relations department deals with three issues of significant importance to women's economic security: access to education, women in the workplace, and retirement security. The "Take Action" portion of the AAUW's website contains useful summaries of the important issues under each of these topics—from Title IX rollbacks to privatization of Social Security—and also "action steps" on how they can be addressed: <http://www.aauw.org/issue_advocacy/actionpages/index.cfm>. AAUW also offers *Action Network*, an e-advocacy program that provides weekly updates on the latest legislative action and a quick, simple way to share your views with Congress. To sign up, visit <http://www.aauw.org/issue_advocacy/ actionnetwork/index.cfm>.

Contact: Lisa Maatz, Director of Public Policy and Government Relations, maatzl@aauw.org

BUSINESS AND PROFESSIONAL WOMEN/USA (BPW/USA)

http://www.bpwusa.org

Business and Professional Women/USA is involved in lobbying on various tax issues, noting the ways in which they negatively or positively affect women. A member of the Fair Taxes for All Coalition, BPW/USA supported legislation signed into law in 2004 to permit civil rights plaintiffs receiving back-wage awards to be taxed over the number of years for which the award was designed to compensate, rather than in a single year. Their current work includes a focus on Social Security and tax-related support for long-term care. They support legislation that would include tax deductions for qualified long-term care insurance and the extension of the Child Tax Credit to those women who care for the elderly, the ill, or those with disabilities.

Contact: Elisabeth Gehl, Director of Public Policy, egehl@bpwusa.org

CENTER FOR POLICY ALTERNATIVES (CPA)

http://www.stateaction.org

In 2000, the Center for Policy Alternatives, along with Lifetime Television for Women, produced an extensive polling and research project on economic policies and priorities for women, titled *Women's Voices 2000.* Some key findings of this report are still relevant nearly five years later. For example, women have urgently and consistently identified juggling time and family and equal pay and benefits as the most dominant economic concerns in their lives. In addition, there has been a shift in women's support for the role government can play in partnering with them to help find solutions for their concerns, with nearly 60 percent of women saying government can and should help. The CPA's 2005 version of its Progressive Agenda series focuses specifically on progressive ways to deal with budget and taxation policy at the state level.

Contact: Bernie Horn, Policy Director, bhorn@cfpa.org

CENTER FOR RESEARCH ON WOMEN, UNIVERSITY OF MEMPHIS

http://cas.memphis.edu/isc/crow

The Center for Research on Women focuses in part on women in low-wage workplaces, particularly in the U.S. South. The Center has published research papers that deal with workplace issues such as the living wage, and race and class differences in women's workplace experiences. All publications are available from their website at <http://cas.memphis.edu/isc/crow/publications.html>. A recent focus at the Center has been the growth of Latino immigration to the South, and the workplace experiences of new immigrants.

Contact: Barbara Ellen Smith, Director, bsmith2@cc.memphis.edu

CENTER FOR THE STUDY OF WOMEN IN SOCIETY, UNIVERSITY OF OREGON

http://csws.uoregon.edu

The Center for the Study of Women in Society, Women in the Northwest Research Initiative, has focused on a host of social policy issues confronting women, most particularly income security and the larger issue of human security. It has published a major study of welfare restructuring in Oregon, *Welfare Restructuring, Work and Poverty* (2002), available online at <http://wnw.uoregon.edu/policymat.shtml>. The Center has also hosted national conferences on welfare (2000) and on human security (2003), and has participated actively in the Council's project on economic security through the involvement of the Center's director, Sandra Morgen, coauthor of this volume and chair of the NCRW Advisory Committee on Economic Security.

Contact: Sandra Morgen, Director, smorgen@uoregon.edu

CENTER FOR WOMEN POLICY STUDIES

http://www.centerwomenpolicy.org

The Center for Women Policy Studies has done substantial research around TANF reauthorization and the effects on women, including research into the positive effects of postsecondary education, which increases women's ability to be self-sustaining once they no longer receive benefits. A report titled *From Poverty to Self-Sufficiency: The Role of Postsecondary Education in Welfare Reform* expands on earlier findings that former TANF recipients with a college education are more likely to stay employed and less likely to return to TANF. The report is available online: <http://www.centerwomenpolicy.org/report_download.cfm?ReportID=75>.

Contact: Leslie Wolfe, President, lwolfe@centerwomenpolicy.org

CENTER FOR WOMEN'S LEADERSHIP, BABSON COLLEGE

http://www.3.babson.edu/cwl

The Center for Women's Leadership at Babson College is working on a project entitled the Impact and Effectiveness of Women's Business Centers, in collaboration with the Association of Women's Business Centers, the National Women's Business Council, and the Level Playing Field Institute. The project surveys Women's Business Centers nationwide to look at the key programs and strategies for potential and active women entrepreneurs. Women's Business Centers were created through Congressional action in the late 1990s and are funded by the Small Business Administration. The report for this project is available online: <http://www.3.babson.edu/cw>.

Contact: Nan Langowitz, Director, langowitz@babson.edu

CENTER FOR WOMEN AND WORK, RUTGERS UNIVERSITY

http://www.rci.rutgers.edu/~cww

The Center for Women and Work researches programs that seek to increase access to education and skills training for low-income single mothers. It assessed a pilot program funded by the New Jersey Department of Labor in which single working low-income mothers received skills training via online learning in their homes. Building on this program, the Center documented an effective way to deliver skills training to an underserved population, finding that online learning democratizes access to education and skills training. The Center, with support from the Alfred P. Sloan Foundation, is working with New Jersey to increase the scale of the project and to implement similar programs both in New Jersey and nationally.

Contacts: Eileen Appelbaum, Director, eappelba@rci.rutgers.edu; Mary Gatta, Director, Workforce Policy and Research, gatta@rci.rutgers.edu

CONSORTIUM ON RACE, GENDER, AND ETHNICITY (CRGE), UNIVERSITY OF MARYLAND, COLLEGE PARK

http://www.crge.umd.edu

The Consortium on Race, Gender, and Ethnicity, with support from the Annie E. Casey Foundation, has produced three Research and Action briefs that document the policies, practices, ideologies, and interactions that produce racial and gender disparities in welfare, education, and civic participation. Current tax policy exacerbates these disparities by weakening social services like welfare and public education. Research and Action briefs offer promising strategies, tools, interventions, and other resources intended to reduce those disparities and suggest several directions for revised social policies. The subjects of these briefs include *Racial, Ethnic and Gender Disparities in Early School Leaving (AKA Dropping Out of School)* and *Racial, Ethnic and Gender Disparities in Access to Jobs, Education and Training Under Welfare Reform.* For copies of these briefs, visit <http://www.crge.umd.edu/research/caseysummary.htm>.

Contacts: Bonnie Thornton Dill, Director, btdill@umd.edu; Amy McLaughlin, Assistant Director, amclaugh@umd.edu; Ruth Zambrana, Graduate Director and Director of Research, rz23@umail.umd.edu

GIRLS INCORPORATED

http://www.girls-inc.org

As consumers and workers, most girls also are taxpayers. At age fourteen, 59 percent of young women had jobs, compared with 55 percent of young men. Yet fewer girls than boys say they are very knowledgeable about finance and money management. Girls Incorporated developed a program to enhance girls' financial competence and confidence, to empower girls to recognize early on that they can exercise control over their financial futures, and to promote within girls a sense of economic justice. Girls Inc. Economic Literacy fosters the development of skills that girls need to make informed decisions. Go to <http://www.girlsinc.org/ic/page.php?id=3> for resources on Girls and Economic Literacy.

Contact: Heather Johnston Nicholson, Director of Research, hjnicholson@girls-inc.org

INSTITUTE FOR TEACHING AND RESEARCH ON WOMEN (ITROW), TOWSON STATE UNIVERSITY

http://www.towson.edu/itrow

Towson's Institute for Teaching and Research on Women is currently developing a program for low-income women, called Pathways. The program will enable greater access to higher education for both low-income students and those receiving TANF, with the ultimate goal of promoting long-term economic self-reliance. ITROW is also involved in debates surrounding social security and women. In April, 2005 ITROW was a cosponsor and organizer, along with the Center for Productive Aging at Towson, of the conference "Women at Risk: The Future of Social Security," an Official White House Conference on Aging event.

Contact: Karen Dugger, Director, kdugger@towson.edu

INSTITUTE FOR WOMEN AND WORK, CORNELL UNIVERSITY

http://www.ilr.cornell.edu/extension/iww/default.html

The Institute for Women and Work is involved in several initiatives that work to further the economic independence of women. The Institute is launching a women's financial literacy campaign, headed by an advisory council of prominent New York women in major financial sectors. In June 2004, they hosted an Asian Women's Business Conference, and in October 2004, a Caribbean and Hispanic Women's Business Association Conference. The Institute is also committed to moving women's economic agendas by encouraging unionization and promoting public policies that address such issues as overtime pay, increasing the minimum wage, and the gender wage gap. The Institute's agenda also recognizes that women are disproportionately affected by federal, state, and municipal cuts in child-care and elder-care provisions for working families, and hosts forums and educational seminars on the status of working families both nationally and internationally.

Contact: Francine Moccio, Director, fam5@cornell.edu

INSTITUTE FOR WOMEN'S POLICY RESEARCH (IWPR)

http://www.iwpr.org

IWPR is a leading national resource on issues that are critical to the economic stability of women, including tax and budget issues, poverty and welfare, employment and earnings, work and family issues, the economic and social aspects of health care and safety, and women's civic and political participation. IWPR's recent work includes: the effect of the recession on women, the effect of federal budget cuts to Medicaid for women, the cost of not providing paid sick leave, women's access to pensions, and the impact of welfare reform on children. IWPR also releases biennial reports on the social, political, and economic status of women in the states. The 2004 Status of Women in the States reports can be accessed online at <http://www.iwpr.org/States2004/SWS2004/index.htm>. IWPR recently launched a new website on the income security of women in retirement and the possible effects of social security privatization on women, online at <http://womenandsocialsecurity.org>. Its new e-mail alert on women and social security is going to thousands of people across the country, who are using it to stay informed on how proposed changes in Social Security, including changes in taxes and benefits, might affect them.

Contacts: Heidi Hartmann, President, hartmann@iwpr.org; Barbara Gault, Director of Research, gault@iwpr.org; Avis Jones-DeWeever, Study Director for Poverty and Welfare, jones-deweever@iwpr.org; Amy Caiazza, Study Director for Democracy and Society, caiazza@iwpr.org; Sunhwa Lee, Study Director for Older Women's Economics, including women and social security, lee@iwpr.org; Vicky Lovell, Study Director for Employment and Earnings and Work and Family, lovell@iwpr.org.

INTERNATIONAL ASSOCIATION FOR FEMINIST ECONOMISTS (IAFFE)

http://www.iaffe.org

The International Association for Feminist Economics (IAFFE) is a nonprofit membership organization that seeks to advance feminist inquiry of economic issues and to educate economists and others on feminist points of view on economic issues. IAFFE has approximately 600 members in 43 countries, including the top feminist economists working in the field. IAFFE publishes a journal, *Feminist Economics*. More information about the journal is available on IAFFE's website.

Contact: Cinda Smith, Executive Director, clsmith@iaffe.org

INTERNATIONAL CENTER FOR RESEARCH ON WOMEN (ICRW)

http://www.icrw.org

In 2003, ICRW was commissioned by the Commonwealth Secretariat, as part of its series of economic policy studies, to write a report, *Gender Impacts of Government Revenue Collection: The Case of Taxation*, available at <http://www.icrw.org/html/projects/projects_poverty.htm>. It reviews the gender dimensions of taxation and makes recommendations to improve gender equity in tax policy in developing countries. ICRW has organized workshops and presentations on this issue for nongovernmental organizations (NGOs) and representatives of international agencies such as the World Bank and the U.S. Agency for International Development. ICRW also developed a module on Gender and Taxation in Developing Countries for the Knowledge Networking Program on Engendering Macroeconomics of the International Working Group on Gender and Macroeconomics based at the University of Utah.

Contact: Kathleen Barnett, Vice President of Programs, kbarnett@icrw.org.

LEGAL MOMENTUM

http://www.legalmomentum.org

Women and Poverty Project: Legal Momentum's Women and Poverty Project focuses on issues related to women's disproportionate poverty, including TANF, domestic violence, child care, and women's rights. Legal Momentum has also created a coalition, the BOB (Building Opportunities Beyond Welfare Reform) Coalition, of hundreds of groups working to end women's poverty. For more information about the coalition, visit <http://www.legalmomentum.org/issues/wel/reastatement.shtml>.

Family Initiative: Legal Momentum's Family Initiative works for strong public investment in child care, preschool, and after-school. The Initiative's goal is to yield solid economic returns—to the children whose school performance and retention are enhanced, to the millions of families for whom care is the most costly item in the household budget after rent, to businesses that experience lower absenteeism and greater productivity, and to communities and states that benefit from job creation, school success, a better-trained workforce, and reduced crime. The Initiative has its own website: http://www.familyinitiative.org.

Contact: Nicole A. Brown, Policy Attorney, nbrown@legalmomentum.org

MS. FOUNDATION FOR WOMEN

http://www.ms.foundation.org

The Ms. Foundation for Women supports the efforts of women and girls to influence the world around them and to control their own lives. The Ms. Foundation is especially interested in the intersections of gender, race, class, age, sexual orientation, immigration status, and ability, which both distinguish and connect every woman's lived experience. The goal of economic stability is a major impetus for much of the work of the Foundation, as is a vision of building a world free from violence. Using a feminist and human rights framework in working on economic security issues across the United States, the Ms. Foundation funds organizations that build the collective power and leadership of women and girls in the workplace and in society at large. The Foundation uses a range of strategies—from supporting groups who advocate for better wages and working conditions to groups who promote programs, policies, and best practices that foster women's business and asset development—all toward the goal of enabling women to support themselves and their families. Among other strategic efforts, the Ms. Foundation is a member and supporter of the Association for Enterprise Opportunity, the Fair Taxes for All Coalition, the Family Economic Self-Sufficiency Standard Coalition, and the Grantmakers Income Security Taskforce. Beyond grantmaking, the foundation also produces books and conducts public education on economic security and economic empowerment.

Contacts: Sara Gould, President & CEO, sgould@ms.foundation.org; Mia White, Program Officer, mwhite@ms.foundation.org

NATIONAL CENTER ON WOMEN AND AGING, BRANDEIS UNIVERSITY

http://www.heller.brandeis.edu/national

The NCWA researches critical issues facing older women today, including Social Security. The Center (which transitioned to a program in late 2005) has looked specifically at the impact on women of raising the age for Medicare benefits, and has completed a series of monographs to examine how privatization will affect women. The monographs present a cross-national comparison of women's experiences in Australia, Great Britain, and the United States, looking specifically at the impact of privatization on retirement funding. *Older Women and Private Pensions in the United Kingdom, Older Women and Private Pensions in Australia,* and *Older Women and Private Pensions in the United States* are available to order from the NCWA website.

Contact: Phyllis H. Mutschler, Executive Director, mutsch1@brandeis.edu

NATIONAL RESEARCH CENTER FOR WOMEN AND FAMILIES

(formerly the National Center for Policy Research on Women and Families)
http://www.center4research.org

The National Research Center for Women and Families examines the implications of tax policies for the health and safety of women, children, and families. Major concerns include the effects of privatization of Social Security on the lives of women, and on children and adults with disabilities; the impact of welfare reform on women, children, and families; and the impact of tax policies on federal and state funding available to improve the quality and availability of health care and child care. Recent papers include *Children and Social Security: So Much More than a Retirement Plan* (Issue Brief) <http://www.center4research.org/sschildren.html>, *Welfare Reform Needs Reform* <http://www.center4research.org/welreform.html>, and *The Evolution of Welfare Reform: Policy Changes and Current Knowledge* <http:// www.center 4research.org/poverty4.html>.

Contact: Diana Zuckerman, President, dz@center4policy.org

NATIONAL WOMEN'S LAW CENTER (NWLC)

http://www.nwlc.org

NWLC works on tax-related issues such as child care and state and federal tax policy, and includes useful information on tax issues on their website: <http://www.nwlc.org/display.cfm?section=tax>. NWLC also publishes updates, press releases, and fact sheets on tax and budget issues and the effects of budget cuts on programs targeting women. NWLC recently published a report titled *Social Security: Women, Children, and the States,* which provides an analysis for each of the 50 states and the District of Columbia about the importance of Social Security to women, children, and the states and the impact of cuts in Social Security benefits that would result from the current proposed privatization plan. The report is available at

<http://www.nwlc. org/pdf/sswomen&states2005.pdf>. NWLC is cochair of the Fair Taxes for All Coalition.

Contact: Joan Entmacher, Vice President and Director of the Family Economic Security Program, jentmacher@nwlc.org

WOMEN AND GENDER IN GLOBAL PERSPECTIVES PROGRAM (WGGP), UNIVERSITY OF ILLINOIS, URBANA-CHAMPAIGN

http://www.ips.uiuc.edu/wggp

The Women and Gender in Global Perspectives Program at the University of Illinois Urbana-Champaign addresses transnational migration and human security issues in much of its work. A current interdisciplinary research project focuses on gender and human security for immigrants in the Midwest, stressing health care, housing, and income security. For example, recent immigrants are usually paying more in taxes than they receive in benefits. In light of the proposed changes in the Social Security system, WGGP is preparing forums and publications on the importance of the insurance (as well as the retirement) function of Social Security and illustrating how women, minorities, and immigrants would be particularly disadvantaged by movement to private accounts. "Gender and Human Security: Latina/o Immigrants in the Midwest," a summary of WGGP's March 2004 symposium, is available online at <http://www.ips.uiuc.edu/wggp/immigration.html>.

Contact: Gale Summerfield, Director, summrfld@uiuc.edu

WOMEN'S INSTITUTE FOR A SECURE RETIREMENT (WISER)

www.wiserwomen.org

WISER is a nonprofit organization whose primary mission is education and advocacy to improve the long-term financial quality of life for women. WISER supports women's opportunities to secure fair pensions and adequate retirement income, through research, workshops, and partnerships. WISER has published landmark reports on the state of women's retirement: *Your Future Paycheck: What Women Need to Know About Pay, Social Security, Pensions, Savings and Investments* and *Minority Women and Retirement Income, Your Future Paycheck.* It also published *What Everybody Needs to Know About Money and Retirement* as an insert in *Good Housekeeping* magazine.

WISER conducts "how-to" training workshops on pensions, savings, investments, retirement health care, long-term care insurance, widowhood, divorce, and Social Security, and also broader education campaigns through the media. It also educates the public through its web-based national clearinghouse on women and retirement. WISER advocates on Capitol Hill for pension improvements, adequate Social Security benefits for women (particularly widows and disabled widows), and tax law changes to promote retirement planning, including a campaign to extend and expand the Saver's Tax Credit.

Contact: Cindy Hounsell, Executive Director, WiserWomen@aol.com

WOMEN'S RESEARCH AND EDUCATION INSTITUTE (WREI)

http://www.wrei.org

WREI addresses women's economic security in several ways. It produces a biannual book, *The American Woman*, which has a large statistical section on women's changing position, including data about their economic position. Its Women in Uniform program is the oldest and largest ongoing program about women in the military among progressive women's centers, and it follows women veterans' health and employment issues. Crossing Borders, an immigration program, follows statistics on employment and, increasingly, on remittances, data that deals with women's economic security. WREI also has a new program on women and religion, Connecting the Dots, which includes information about women in relation to family obligations and religious behavior that touches on economic security.

Contact: Susan Scanlan, President, scanlan@wrei.org

OTHER ORGANIZATIONS WORKING ON TAX ISSUES

CENTER ON BUDGET AND POLICY PRIORITIES

http://www.cbpp.org

The Center on Budget and Policy Priorities focuses on policy and budget issues that affect low- and moderate-income people. The Center works on many areas of particular concern to women, such as: the Child Tax Credit, health policies, housing, immigration, social security, and TANF reauthorization.

CITIZENS FOR TAX JUSTICE (CTJ)

http://www.ctj.org

Citizens for Tax Justice focuses on federal, state, and local tax policies and their impact upon our nation. CTJ advocates for many of the issues highlighted in this book.

COUNCIL ON CONTEMPORARY FAMILIES

http://www.contemporaryfamilies.org

The Council on Contemporary Families is a national organization made up of noted family researchers, mental health and social work practitioners, and clinicians dedicated to enhancing the national conversation about what contemporary families need and how these needs can best be met. On April 15, 2005, the Council released a report by Rachel Henneck, titled *Value for Family Tax Dollars: How Does the U.S. Stack Up?*

FAIR TAXES FOR ALL

http://www.fairtaxes4all.org

Fair Taxes for All is a coalition made up of 325 member organizations, fighting to ensure that federal resources from taxes go toward the things that matter most: schools, health care, fire protection, child care, and much more. Of their member centers, many are also members of the National Council for Research on Women, including:

- American Association of University Women
- Business and Professional Women/USA
- Center for Women Policy Studies
- Legal Momentum
- National Women's Law Center
- Ms. Foundation for Women
- Women Employed Institute
- YWCA U.S.A.

NATIONAL COUNCIL OF WOMEN'S ORGANIZATIONS (NCWO), DOMESTIC PRIORITIES TASK FORCE

http://www.womensorganizations.org

The work of the Domestic Priorities Task Force is in support of NCWO's Policy Agenda. Some key issues of concern are workplace and economic equity, tax equity, child care and early education, and Social Security.

NATIONAL GAY AND LESBIAN TASK FORCE

http://www.thetaskforce.org/index.cfm

The National Gay and Lesbian Task Force works to build the grassroots political power of the LGBT (lesbian, gay, bisexual, and transgendered) community to win complete equality. The Policy Institute at the Task Force publishes on economic and racial justice, welfare reform, family, and elder/senior issues as they affect the LGBT community.

TAX POLICY CENTER: A JOINT VENTURE OF THE URBAN INSTITUTE AND BROOKINGS INSTITUTION

http://www.taxpolicycenter.org/home

Tax Policy Center staff publish in a variety of outlets about a wide range of tax issues, including *Taxes, the Budget and Economy; Tax Reform; Taxation of Households, Savings, Wealth and Retirement*; and *Government and Philanthropy*. All publications are available on the Tax Policy Center website. The website also features "tax facts" and "tax breaks" columns. Research reports from the Center appear in nationally respected journals and researchers contribute to the policy brief series of its constituent organizations, the Urban Institute (http://www.urban.org) and Brookings Institution (http://www.brookings.org).

UNITED FOR A FAIR ECONOMY (UFE)

http://www.faireconomy.org

United for a Fair Economy works for economic justice, raising awareness that "concentrated wealth and power undermine the economy, corrupt democracy, deepen the racial divide, and tear communities apart." Recent work by UFE has focused on income disparity, the racial underpinnings of the gap between the rich and poor, and the tax system's shift from taxing corporations and the upper class to the middle and working classes.

WOMEN'S ACTION FOR NEW DIRECTIONS (WAND)

http://www.wand.org

The WAND Education Fund works to educate the public about the need to reduce violence and militarism, and has composed several useful fact sheets that explain the budget process in easy to understand terms. Fact sheets are available online, and include *The American Pie Experience* <http://www.wand.org/getfacts/index/ampie_05_3a.pdf> and *All Our Dollars: A Guide to Budget Terms* <http://www.wand.org/getfacts/ index/dollars03_3>.

WOMEN'S SOCIAL POLICY & RESEARCH CENTER, VANDERBILT UNIVERSITY (W-SPARC)

http://www.sitemason.vanderbilt.edu/wsparc

W-SPARC has conducted a number of studies on taxes and other issues important to women's economic security. In two studies, *Tax Reform and Tennessee Households: A Distributional Impact Analysis* and *Footing the Bill: Women and Tax Reform in Tennessee*, W-SPARC looked at the potential impact on Tennessee women and households of tax change scenarios under consideration by the state legislature, relative to the impact of the status quo sales tax system. The results of both studies show the disproportionate tax bill that Tennessee women pay, and illustrate the need for a progressive state income tax, elimination of the tax on groceries, and a state Earned Income Tax Credit. W-SPARC is currently working on *Women, Minorities and Federal Income Taxes*, an analysis of the distributional impact of the federal tax system on women and minorities, with Professor Beverly Moran of Vanderbilt Law School. Other W-SPARC projects related to women's economic security include studies on the gender composition of corporate leadership in Tennessee's public companies, immigrant women and work in Tennessee, scholarships and other resources for Tennessee women, and the impact on women of health insurance loss and health-care reforms in Tennessee.

APPENDIX B: LIST OF NATIONAL COUNCIL FOR RESEARCH ON WOMEN MEMBER CENTERS

ARIZONA

University of Arizona, Southwest Institute for Research on Women

CALIFORNIA

Mills College, Women's Leadership Institute
Stanford University, Institute for Research on Women and Gender
University of California, Berkeley, Beatrice M. Bain Research Group
University of California, Davis
   Chicana/Latina Research Center
   Consortium for Women and Research
University of California, Los Angeles
   Center for the Study of Women
   Higher Education Research Institute
University of Southern California, Center for Feminist Research

COLORADO

University of Denver, Higher Education Resource Services, Mid-America

DISTRICT OF COLUMBIA

American Association of University Women Educational Foundation

American Council on Education, Office of Women in Higher Education
American University, Women and Politics Institute
Association of American Colleges and Universities, Program on the Status and Education
    of Women
Business and Professional Women's Foundation
Center for Policy Alternatives
Center for Women Policy Studies
George Washington University, Women's Studies Program
Howard University, African American Women's Institute
Institute for Women's Policy Research
International Center for Research on Women
National Research Center for Women and Families
National Council of Negro Women
National Women's Law Center
Society for Women's Health Research
Women's Institute for a Secure Retirement
Women's Research and Education Institute
Young Women's Christian Association of the USA

FLORIDA

University of Florida, Center for Women's Studies and Gender Research

GEORGIA

Georgia Institute of Technology, Center for the Study of Women, Science, and Technology
Spelman College, Women's Research and Resource Center

IDAHO

Boise State University, Gender Studies Program

ILLINOIS

Loyola University, Gannon Center for Women and Leadership
University of Illinois at Chicago, Center for Research on Women and Gender
University of Illinois at Urbana-Champaign, Women and Gender in Global Perspectives
    Program

INDIANA

Girls Incorporated, National Resource Center
St. Mary's College, Notre Dame, Center for Women's InterCultural Leadership

LOUISIANA

Tulane University, Newcomb Center for Research on Women

MAINE

University of New England, Women's Center for Ethics in Action

MARYLAND

National Women's Studies Association
Towson State University, Institute for Teaching and Research on Women
University of Maryland, College Park, Consortium on Race, Gender, and Ethnicity

MASSACHUSETTS

Babson College, Center for Women's Leadership
Brandeis University
    Hadassah Brandeis Institute
    Women's Studies Research Center
Harvard University
    Kennedy School, Women and Public Policy Program
    Radcliffe Institute for Advanced Study
Mt. Holyoke College, Five Colleges Women's Studies Research Center
Simmons School of Management, Center for Gender in Organizations
Smith College, Project on Women and Social Change
University of Massachusetts, Boston, Center for Women in Politics and Public Policy
Wellesley College, Wellesley Centers for Women

MICHIGAN

University of Michigan
    Center for the Education of Women
    Institute for Research on Women and Gender

MINNESOTA

College of St. Catherine, Abigail Quigley McCarthy Center for Women
University of Minnesota, Humphrey Institute, Center on Women and Public Policy

NEVADA

University of Nevada, Las Vegas, Women's Research Institute of Nevada

NEW JERSEY

Rutgers University
    Center for the American Woman and Politics, Eagleton Institute of Politics
    Center for Women and Work
    Center for Women's Global Leadership
    Institute for Research on Women
    Institute for Women's Leadership

NEW YORK

Association of Junior Leagues International
Barnard College, Barnard Center for Research on Women
Catalyst
CUNY Graduate School and University, Center for the Study of Women and Society
Columbia University, Institute for Research on Women and Gender
Cornell University, Institute on Women and Work
Feminist Press at the City University of New York
Girl Scouts of the USA
Girls Incorporated
Hadassah
Hamilton College, The Kirkland Project
Hobart and William Smith Colleges, The Fisher Center for the Study of Women and Men
Hunter College, Center for the Study of Family Policy
Legal Momentum
Marymount College Tarrytown, Institute for the Education of Women and Girls
Ms. Foundation for Women
New York University, Center for the Study of Gender and Sexuality
Planned Parenthood Federation of America
SUNY, Albany
    Center for Women in Government and Civil Society
    Institute for Research on Women
SUNY, Binghamton, Women's Studies Program
SUNY, Buffalo, Institute for Research and Education on Women and Gender
Women's Interart Center
The White House Project

NORTH CAROLINA

Duke University, Women's Studies Program

OHIO

Kent State University, Project on the Study of Gender and Education
Ohio State University, Department of Women's Studies
University of Cincinnati, Center for Women's Studies

OREGON

University of Oregon, Center for the Study of Women in Society

PENNSYLVANIA

University of Pennsylvania, Alice Paul Center for Research on Women and Gender

RHODE ISLAND

Brown University, Pembroke Center for Teaching and Research on Women

TENNESSEE

University of Memphis, Center for Research on Women

TEXAS

University of Texas, Austin, Center for Women's and Gender Studies

UTAH

Brigham Young University, Women's Research Institute
University of Utah, Women's Resource Center
Utah State University, Women and Gender Research Institute

VIRGINIA

The Feminist Majority Foundation
International Association for Feminist Economics
Radford University, Center for Gender Studies
Virginia Tech, Science and Gender Equity Program

WASHINGTON

Washington State University, Women's Resource Center

WISCONSIN

University of Wisconsin, Madison, Women's Studies Research Center

INTERNATIONAL

Flacso, Argentina, Area of Gender, Society and Policies

NOTES

1 WHO ARE WOMEN TAXPAYERS AND WHAT DO THEY NEED TO KNOW?

1. Ellen Yau, Kurt Gurka, and Peter Sailer (1999), *Comparing Salaries and Wages of Women Shown on Forms W-2 to Those of Men, 1969–1999*, U.S. Internal Revenue Service, Statistics of Income Division: <http://www.irs.gov/pub/irs-soi/99inw2wm.pdf>.

2. Eileen Appelbaum, et al. (2004), *The Minimum Wage and Working Women*, June 18, Center for Women and Work, Rutgers University: <http://www.cww.rutgers.edu/dataPages/minwagewomen6-18-04.pdf>.

3. Stephen Rose and Heidi Hartmann (2004), *Still a Man's Labor Market: The Long-Term Earnings Gap*, Institute for Women's Policy Research: *<http://www.iwpr.org/pdf/ C355.pdf>*.

4. U.S. General Accounting Office (2002), *Women in Management: An Analysis of Current Population Survey Data:* <http://www.gao.gov/new.items/d02648t.pdf>.

5. National Women's Law Center (2004), "NWLC Analysis of New Census Data Finds Poverty of Women and Children Increases for Third Straight Year," news release (August 26): <http://www.nwlc.org/details.cfm?id=1986&section=newsroom>.

6. Stephen Rose and Heidi Hartmann (2004), *Still a Man's Labor Market: The Long-Term Earnings Gap*, Institute for Women's Policy Research: <http://www.iwpr.org/pdf/ C355.pdf>.

7. National Women's Law Center (2005), "New Census Data Show Women's Poverty Increases for Fourth Year, Women's Wages Decrease, Despite Economic Recovery," news release (August 30): <http://www.nwlc.org/details.cfm?id=2385&section=newsroom>.

8. ACNielsen Company (2005), "Large Number of U.S. Consumers Continuing to Live Paycheck to Paycheck," survey results (June 13) <http://us.acnielsen.com/news/20050613.shtml>.

9. Women's Institute for a Secure Retirement (2002), "Some Statistics from *Your Future Paycheck*": <http://www.wiser.heinz.org/paycheckpoints.html>.

10. Cynthia Costello, Vanessa Wight, and Anne Stone, eds., for the Women's Research and Education Institute (2003), *The American Woman 2003–2004: Daughters of a Revolution: Young Women Today* (New York: Palgrave Macmillan), 155.

11. Women's Institute for a Secure Retirement (2005), *Minority Women and Retirement Income*, Your Future Paycheck series (April): <http://www.wiser.heinz.org/wiserminorityApr05. pdf>.

12. National Women's Law Center (2005), "New Census Data Show Women's Poverty Increases for Fourth Year, Women's Wages Decrease, Despite Economic Recovery," news release (August 30): <http://www.nwlc.org/details.cfm?id=2385&section=newsroom>.

13. Misha Werschkul and Erica Williams (2004), *The Status of Women in the States*, Institute for Women's Policy Research, 32: <http://www.iwpr.org/States2004/PDFs/ National.pdf>.

14. Misha Werschkul and Erica Williams (2004), *The Status of Women in the States*, Institute for Women's Policy Research, 60: <http://www.iwpr.org/States2004/PDFs/National.pdf>.

15. Ellen Yau, Kurt Gurka, and Peter Sailer (1999), *Comparing Salaries and Wages of Women Shown on Forms W-2 to Those of Men, 1969–1999*, U.S. Internal Revenue Service, Statistics of Income Division: <http://www.irs.gov/pub/irs-soi/99inw2wm.pdf>.

16. Ibid.

17. Consumer Federation of America (2004), "Research Shows That Women on Their Own Face Financial Challenges," news release (January 12): <http://www.consumerfed.org/women-finance.pdf>.

18. Misha Werschkul and Erica Williams (2004), *The Status of Women in the States*, Institute for Women's Policy Research, 60: <http://www.iwpr.org/States2004/PDFs/National.pdf>.

19. Ibid.

20. Melody Slashinski for Girls, Incorporated (2004), "Girls and Taxes: Fast Facts" presented at "Women's Voices Matter: Women Elect to Speak," annual conference of the National Council for Research on Women, June 6–7, Washington, D.C.

21. Packaged Fact, Inc. (2002), "The U.S. Teens Market: Understanding the Changing Lifestyles and Trends of 12- to 19-Year Olds," *Market Research.com,* <http://www.market research.com/map/prod/746398.html>.

22. Melody Slashinski for Girls, Incorporated (2004), "Girls and Taxes: Fast Facts" presented at "Women's Voices Matter: Women Elect to Speak," annual conference of the National Council for Research on Women, June 6–7, Washington, D.C.

23. Misha Werschkul and Erica Williams (2004), *The Status of Women in the States*, Institute for Women's Policy Research, 58: <http://www.iwpr.org/States2004/PDFs/National.pdf>.

24. Gaydemographics.org (2002), "PUMS [Public Use Microdata Sample], Same-Sex Couples," based on data from U.S. Census Bureau, 2000 Census: <http://www.gaydemograph-ics.org/USA/PUMS/nationalintro.htm>.

25. U.S. Department of Health and Human Services, Office of Women's Health, National Women's Health Information Center (2005), "Illness and Disability" page, womenshealth.gov: <http://www.4woman.gov/wwd>.

26. Julia E. Bradsher (1996), *Disability Among Racial and Ethnic Groups*, Disability Statistics Abstract 10 (January), Disability Statistics Rehabilitation Research and Training Center,

University of California, San Francisco/U.S. Department of Education, National Institute on Disability and Rehabilitation Research, <http://dsc.ucsf.edu/pdf/abstract10.pdf>.

27. Institute for Women's Policy Research (2005), *Who Are Social Security Beneficiaries?*, Fact Sheet (March) <http://womenandsocialsecurity.org/Women_Social_Security/pdf/D461.pdf>.

28. Ibid.

29. U.S. Social Security Administration (2005), "Current-Pay Benefits: Disabled Workers, December 2003," *Annual Statistical Supplement, 2004:* <http://www.ssa.gov/policy/docs/stat-comps/supplement/2004/5d.pdf>.

30. L. Jans and S. Stoddard (1999), *Chartbook on Women and Disability in the United States,* InfoUse Report, U.S. National Institute on Disability and Rehabilitation Research: <http://www.infouse.com/disabilitydata/womendisability/3_6.php>.

31. Carmen DeNavas-Walt, Bernadette D. Proctor, and Robert J. Mills (2004), *Income, Poverty, and Health Insurance Coverage in the United States: 2003,* U.S. Census Bureau, Current Population Reports: <http://www.census.gov/prod/2004pubs/p60-226.pdf>.

32. National Immigration Law Center (2005), "Overview of Immigrant Eligibility for Federal Programs," *Guide to Immigrant Eligibility for Federal Programs,* 4th ed., Table 1: <http://www.nilc.org/pubs/guideupdates/tbl1_ovrvw_fed_pgms_032505.pdf>.

33. Amy Caiazza (2002), *The Status of Women in the States,* Institute for Women's Policy Research, 38: <http://www.iwpr.org/states2002/>.

34. Republican National Committee (2004), "Setting the Record Straight: President Bush's Tax Cuts Reduce Burden on the Middle Class": <http://www.georgewbush.com/Economy/Read.aspx?ID=3283>.

35. Annette Bernhardt, Laura Dresser, and Catherine Hill (2000), *Why Privatizing Government Services Would Hurt Women Workers,* Research-in-Brief, Institute for Women's Policy Research: <http://www.iwpr.org/pdf/b237.pdf>.

36. U.S. Department of Labor, Women's Bureau (2003), *20 Leading Occupations of Women,* based on data from Bureau of Labor Statistics: <http://www.dol.gov/wb/factsheets/20lead2003_txt.htm>.

2   TAX TALK 101: WHAT GETS TAXED, WHY, AND HOW?

1. Paul M. Johnson (2005), *A Glossary of Political Economy Terms,* web page of Dr. Paul M. Johnson, Auburn University, <http://www.auburn.edu/~johnspm/gloss/index.html>.

2. Ibid.

3. Tax Foundation (2005), *America Celebrates Tax Freedom Day,* Special Report 134 (April): <http://www.taxfoundation.org/files/8ae0ffb685f381da2b2fc6d035513ac7.pdf>.

4. Nancy Folbre (2002), *The Invisible Heart: Economics and Family Values* (New York: The New Press).

5. U.S. Office of Management and Budget (2004), *Budget of the United States Government, Fiscal Year 2005,* Summary Tables, Table S-1: Budget Totals: <http://www.whitehouse.gov/omb/budget/fy2005/tables.html>.

6. Nancy Folbre (2004), presentation at "Women's Voices Matter: Women Elect to Speak," annual conference of the National Council for Research on Women, 6–7 June 2004, Washington, D.C.

7. Adam Smith (1776), *An Inquiry into the Nature and Causes of the Wealth of Nations* (New York: Random House, 1937).

8. Richard Kogan and Robert Greenstein (2004), *Official Treasury Report Shows Fourth Year of Deficit Growth Despite Economic Recovery* (October 4), Center on Budget and Policy Priorities: <http://www.cbpp.org/10-14-04bud.htm>.

9. U.S. Office of Management and Budget (2005), *Budget of the United States Government, Fiscal Year 2006*, Historical Tables, Tables 13 and 7.1: <http://www.whitehouse.gov/omb/budget/fy2006/pdf/hist.pdf>.

10. Martha Covan and Richard Kogan (2004), *Introduction to the Federal Budget Process* (December 29), Center on Budget and Policy Priorities: <http://www.cbpp.org/3-7-03bud.htm>.

11. Edward McCaffrey (2003), *Marriage Penalty Relief in New Tax Law*, Brief Analysis No. 445, National Center for Policy Analysis: <http://www.ncpa.org/pub/ba/ba445>.

12. Elizabeth Cady Stanton, et al., eds. (1881). *History of Woman Suffrage*, Vol. 2 (New York: Arno Press, 1969).

13. Susan Peck Fowler (1907), Letter to *Vineland Evening News*, New Jersey (December 16).

14. Center for American Women and Politics, Rutgers University (2004), *Women in Elective Office 2004*, Fact Sheet: <http://www.cawp.rutgers.edu/Facts/Officeholders/elective.pdf>.

3 WOMEN AND TAXES: WE *ALL* COULD (AND DO) USE HELP

1. *See* Mimi Abramovitz (1983). "Everyone's s on Welfare: The Role of Redistribution in Social Policy—Revisited. *Social Work* 28:6 (November/December), 440–45; Lois Bryson (1992), *Welfare and the State: Who Benefits?* (New York: St. Martin Press); and Christopher Howard (1997), *The Hidden Welfare State: Tax Expenditures and Social Policy in the United States* (Princeton, N.J.: Princeton University Press).

2. U.S. Congress, Joint Committee on Taxation (2005), *Estimates of Federal Tax Expenditures for Fiscal Years 2005–2009* (January): <http://www.house.gov/jct/s-1-05.pdf>.

3. Elaine Maag (2004) "Relationship Between Tax Entry Thresholds and Poverty," *Tax Facts* (March 15), Urban-Brookings Tax Policy Center: <http://taxpolicycenter.org/UploadedPDF/1000625_TaxFacts_031504.pdf>.

4. Joseph Llobrera and Bob Zahradnik (2004), *A Hand Up: How State Earned Income Tax Credits Help Working Families Escape Poverty in 2004* (May 14), Center on Budget and Policy Priorities: <http://www.cbpp.org/5-14-04sfp.htm>.

5. Ibid.

6. Kaiser Family Foundation (2004), *Women's Health Policy Facts: Women's Health Insurance Coverage*, Fact Sheet (November): <http://www.kff.org/womenshealth/loader.cfm?url=/commonspot/security/getfile.cfm&PageID=48660>.

7. Older Women's League (2002), *Social Security Privatization: A False Promise for Women*, 2002 Mother's Day Report: <http://www.owl-national.org/owlreports/MothersDay2002.pdf>.

8. National Low-Income Housing Coalition (2004), *2005 Advocates' Guide to Housing and Community Development Policy*, "Public Housing": <http://www.nlihc.org/advocates/publichousing.htm>.

9. Thomas M. Shapiro (2004), *The Hidden Cost of Being African American: How Wealth Perpetuates Inequality* (New York: Oxford University Press), 135.

10. Nancy Folbre (2004), presentation at "Women's Voices Matter: Women Elect to Speak," annual conference of the National Council for Research on Women, 6–7 June 2004, Washington, D.C.

11. U.S. Census Bureau (2003), *School Enrollment 2000*, Census Brief (August): <http://www.census.gov/prod/2003pubs/c2kbr-26.pdf>.

12. Applied Research Center (1998), *Public Schools in the United States: Still Separate, Still Unequal:* <http://www.arc.org/Pages/ArcPub.html>.

13. U.S. Social Security Administration (2004), *Women and Social Security*, Press Office Fact Sheet (September), SocialSecurityOnline: <http://www.ssa.gov/pressoffice/factsheets/women.htm>.

14. U.S. Social Security Administration (2003), "Old Age, Survivors and Disability Insurance," *Annual Statistical Supplement*, Table 6.A2: <http://www.ssa.gov/policy/docs/statcomps/supplement/2003/6a.html#table6.a2>.

15. National Women's Law Center (2005), *Privatizing Social Security: What's at Stake for Women* (January 14): <http://www.nwlc.org/pdf/WhatsAtStakeSocSec1-13-05.pdf>.

16. Mimi Abramovitz (2001), "Everyone is Still on Welfare: The Role of Redistribution in Social Policy," *Social Work* 46:4 (July/August), 299.

17. U.S. Social Security Administration (2004), *Women and Social Security*, Press Office Fact Sheet (September), SocialSecurityOnline: <http://www.ssa.gov/pressoffice/factsheets/women.htm>.

18. Thomas M. Shapiro (2004), *The Hidden Cost of Being African American: How Wealth Perpetuates Inequality* (New York: Oxford University Press), 135.

19. Susan Rees, McAuley Institute (2003), "Women and Housing: A Status Report," *Step Up* 7:2 <http://www.housingall.com/STEPUP/Women_Housing.htm>.

20. Population Reference Bureau (2002), *Homeownership Rates Divide Racial and Ethnic Groups* (October): <http://www.prb.org/AmeristatTemplate.cfm?Section=RaceandEthnicity&template=/ContentManagement/ContentDisplay.cfm&ContentID=7820>.

21. Children's Defense Fund (2004), *The State of America's Children, 2004* (Washington, D.C.: Children's Defense Fund), 14: <http://www.cdfwebstore.com/online-store/scstore/Greenbook2004.pdf>.

22. Linda Faye Williams (2003). *The Constraint of Race : Legacies of White Skin Privilege in America* (University Park: Pennsylvania State University Press), 347.

23. Ibid.

24. Ibid.

25. Ibid.

26. Ibid.

27. Len Burman and Laura Wheaton (2005), "Who Gets the Child Tax Credit?" *Tax Notes* (October 17), The Urban-Brookings Tax Policy Center: <www.taxpolicycenter.org/uploadedPDF/411232_child_tax_credit.pdf>.

28. This number was calculated by including spending for the following non-means-tested programs: all domestic discretionary programs, Social Security, Medicare, Unemployment Compensation, veterans/military retirement, and disability programs. Primary data from U.S. Congressional Budget Office (2004), *The Budget and Economic Outlook: Fiscal Years 2005–2014*, Table 3-6: CBO's Baseline Projections of Mandatory Spending, Including Offsetting Receipts: <http://www.cbo.gov/showdoc.cfm?index=4985&sequence=0>.

29. This number was calculated by including spending for the following means-tested programs: Medicaid, Supplemental Security Income, Food Stamps, Family Support (including TANF), Child Nutrition, student loans, State Children's Health Insurance, and social services. Primary data from U.S. Congressional Budget Office (2004), *The Budget and Economic Outlook: Fiscal Years 2005–2014*, Table 3-6: CBO's Baseline Projections of Mandatory Spending, Including Offsetting Receipts: <http://www.cbo.gov/showdoc.cfm?index=4985&sequence=0>.

30. U.S. Congressional Budget Office (2004), *The Budget and Economic Outlook: Fiscal Years 2005–2014*, Table 3-6: CBO's Baseline Projections of Mandatory Spending, Including Offsetting Receipts: <http://www.cbo.gov/showdoc.cfm?index=4985&sequence=0>.

31. Center for Community Change, Center for Economic and Policy Research, and National Low Income Housing Coalition (2005), *The Crisis in America's Housing: Confronting Myths and Promoting a Balanced Housing Policy:* <http://www.nlihc.org/research/housingmyths.pdf>.

32. National Women's Law Center (2005), "New Census Data Show Women's Poverty Increases for Fourth Year, Women's Wages Decrease, Despite Economic Recovery," news release (August 30): <http://www.nwlc.org/details.cfm?id=2385&section=newsroom>.

33. Isaac Shapiro and Robert Greenstein (2005), *Cuts to Low Income Programs May Far Exceed the Contribution of These Programs to Deficit's Return* (February 9), Center on Budget and Policy Priorities <http://www.cbpp.org/2-4-05bud.pdf>.

34. Robert Greenstein, Joel Friedman, and Isaac Shapiro (2005), *Two Tax Cuts Primarily Benefiting Millionaires Slated to Take Effect in January,* (September 19), Center for Budget and Policy Priorities <http://www.cbpp.org/9-19-05tax.pdf>.

35. U.S. Congress, Joint Committee on Taxation (2005), *Estimates of Federal Tax Expenditures for Fiscal Years 2005–2009* (January): <http://www.house.gov/jct/s-1-05.pdf>.

4 HOW WE GOT HERE: A BRIEF HISTORY OF U.S. TAX POLICY

1. Ellen Yau, Kurt Gurka, and Peter Sailer (1999), *Comparing Salaries and Wages of Women Shown on Forms W-2 to Those of Men, 1969–1999,* U.S. Internal Revenue Service, Statistics of Income Division: <http://www.irs.gov/pub/irs-soi/99inw2wm.pdf>.

2. U.S. Department of the Treasury (2005), "History of the U.S. Tax System," *Fact Sheets: Taxes:* <http://www.treas.gov/education/fact-sheets/taxes/ustax.shtml>.

3. Ibid.

4. Carolyn C. Jones (1988). "Class Tax to Mass Tax: The Role of Propaganda in the Expansion of the Income Tax during World War II," *Buffalo Law Review* (Fall 1988/89) 685–737. *See also* Tax History Project (2003), "Our Fiscal Nonagenarian: The Income Tax Turns 90: <http://www.taxhistory.org/thp/readings.nsf/0/086fb0e51b9a551485256e430076bccb?OpenDocument>.

5. David Cay Johnston (2003), *Perfectly Legal: The Covert Campaign to Rig Our Tax System to Benefit the Super Rich —and Cheat Everyone Else* (New York: Portfolio), 16–19.

6. Ibid.

7. Robert McIntyre (1984), *Just Taxes and Other Options.* Citizens for Tax Justice: <http://www.ctj.org/pdf/justtax.pdf>.

8. Ibid.

9. Julianne Malveaux (2004), presentation at "Women's Voices Matter: Women Elect to

Speak," annual conference of the National Council for Research on Women, June 6–7, Washington, D.C.

10. Marty Liebowitz (2003), *Winning Responses to Tough Tax Questions*, United for a Fair Economy (May 12): <http://www.ufenet.org/econ/state/Talking_Taxes>; and Urban-Brookings Tax Policy Center (2004), *Tax Facts, Corporate/Tables: Historical Top Bracket and Rate:* <http://www.taxpolicycenter.org/TaxFacts/tfdb/TFTemplate.cfm?topic2id=70>.

11. Marty Liebowitz (2003), *Winning Responses to Tough Tax Questions*, United For A Fair Economy (May 12): <http://www.ufenet.org/econ/state/Talking_Taxes>.

12. U.S. Congressional Budget Office (2004), *Effective Federal Tax Rates Under Current Law, 2001 to 2014:* <http://www.cbo.gov/showdoc.cfm?index=5746&sequence=1&from=0>.

13. U.S. General Accounting Office (1994), *Tax Policy: Tax Expenditures Deserve More Scrutiny* (Washington, D.C.: U.S. GAO).

14. Robert McIntyre (1996), *Tax Expenditures: The Hidden Entitlements Citizens for Tax Justice:* <http://www.ctj.org/hid_ent/contents/content.htm>, especially "Tax Expenditures, Fiscal 1996–2002, A Detailed List": <http://www.ctj.org/pdf/hideapp1.pdf>.

15. U.S. Congress, Joint Committee on Taxation (2005), *Estimates of Federal Tax Expenditures for Fiscal Years 2005–2009* (January): <http://www.house.gov/jct/s-1-05.pdf>.

16. Allan Sloan (2004), "Why Your Tax Cut Doesn't Add Up," *Newsweek* (April 12): <http://www.msnbc.msn.com/id/4678768/site/newsweek>.

17. Edward Wolff (1996), *Top Heavy: The Increasing Inequality of Wealth in America and What Can Be Done About It* (New York: The New Press), 1–3.

18. Ibid.

19. United for a Fair Economy (2004), *A History of the Estate Tax*, Estate Tax Action Center Fact Sheet: <http://www.faireconomy.org/estatetax/ETHistory.html>.

20. Ibid.

21. Edward Wolff (1996), *Top Heavy: The Increasing Inequality of Wealth in America and What Can Be Done About It* (New York: The New Press), 34.

22. Francisco Perez-González (2003), *Large Shareholders and Dividends: Evidence From U.S. Tax Returns:* <http://www.columbia.edu/~fp2010/lgsh.pdf>.

23. Chuck Collins, Chris Hartman, Karen Kraut, and Gloribell Mota (2004), *Shifty Tax Cuts: How They Move the Tax Burden Off the Rich and onto Everyone Else*, United for a Fair Economy: <http://www.faireconomy.org/Taxes/HTMLReports/Shifty_Tax_Cuts.html>.

24. Joel Friedman (2003), *Who Belongs To the "Investor" Class?* (January 23) Center on Budget and Policy Priorities: <http://www.cbpp.org/1-6-03tax2.htm>.

25. Leonoard Burman and David L Gunter (2003), "17 Percent of Families Have Stock Dividends," Tax Notes (May 23), Urban-Brookings Tax Policyan Institute [online]: <http://www.urban.org/UploadedPDF/1000488>.

26. John Springer (2003), *Dividend Tax Cut: Ineffective Stimulus Now, Bigger Deficits Later* (January 23), Center on Budget and Policy Priorities: <http://www.cbpp.org/1-10-03tax.htm>.

27. Bruce Bartlett (2000), "Estate Tax: History Versus Myth," National Center for Policy Analysis: <http://www.ncpa.org/pi/taxes/pd071900b.html> and United for a Fair Economy (2004), *A History of the Estate Tax*, Estate Tax Action Center Fact Sheet: <http://www.faireconomy.org/estatetax/ETHistory.html>.

28. Joel Friedman and Andrew Lee (2002), *Permanent Repeal of the Estate Tax Would Be Costly, Yet Would Benefit Only a Very Few Large Estates* (June 17), Center on Budget and Policy Priorities: <http://www.cbpp.org/6-17-03tax.htm>.

29. Chuck Collins and Lee Farris (2005), *Estate Tax Reform Proposal: United for a Fair Economy Position Submitted to the President's Advisory Panel on Federal Tax Reform*, 4/29/05 (May 23), United for a Fair Economy: <http://www.faireconomy.org/estatetax/latest_news.html>.

30. U.S. Congress, Joint Committee on Taxation (2005), "Estimated Revenue Effects of H.R. 8, The 'Death Tax Repeal Permanency Act of 2005,'": <www.house.gov/jct/x-20-05.pdf>.

31. Jennifer Roback Morse (2002), *Issue Paper on the Death Tax*, Special Report (May 13), Independent Women's Forum: <http://www.iwf.org/specialreports/specrpt_detail.asp?ArticleID =421>.

32. John Springer (2003), *Estate Tax Affects Very Few Family Businesses* (June 17), Center on Budget and Policy Priorities: <http://www.cbpp.org/6-17-03tax-fact2.htm>.

33. Rosie Hunter and Chuck Collins (2003), "Death Tax Deception," *Dollars and Sense* (January/February): <http://www.dollarsandsense.org/archives/2003/0103hunter.html>.

34. Findings based on a national survey of 1,000 likely voters conducted by Greenberg Quinlan Rosner Research on May 6–9, 2002; subject to a margin of error of +/- 3.1 percent: <http://www.ombwatch.org/estatetax/afet_article.phtml?ombfile=http://www.ombwatch.org/ article/articleview/811/1/125?TopicID=1>.

35. Chuck Collins, Chris Hartman, Karen Kraut, and Gloribell Mota (2004), *Shifty Tax Cuts: How They Move the Tax Burden off the Rich and onto Everyone Else*, United for a Fair Economy: <http://www.faireconomy.org/Taxes/HTMLReports/Shifty_Tax_Cuts.html>.

36. Cited in Joel Friedman (2003), *The Decline of Corporate Income Tax Revenues* (October 24), Center for Budget and Policy Priorities: <http://www.cbpp.org/10-16-03tax.htm#fig%204>.

37. U.S. General Accounting Office (2004), *Tax Administration: Comparison of the Reported Tax Liabilities of Foreign- and U.S.-Controlled Corporations, 1996–2000*, Report to Congressional Requesters, GAO-04-358 (February): <http://www.unclefed.com/GAOReports/d04358.pdf>.

38. Citizens for Tax Justice (2003), *More Corporate Tax Shelters on the Way?* (October 14): <http://www.ctj.org/pdf/corp1003.pdf>.

39. U.S. Congressional Budget Office (2004), *The Budget and Economic Outlook: Fiscal Years 2005–2014*, Chapter 4: *<http://www.cbo.gov/showdoc.cfm?index=6060&sequence=5>*.

40. Richard Kogan and Isaac Shapiro (2005), *Revenue Collections in 2005: What Does the Recent Increase in Revenues Signify?* (July 12), Center for Budget and Policy Priorities: <http://www.cbpp.org/7-12-05bud.htm>.

41. U.S. Executive Office of the President (2001), *Budget of the United States Government, Fiscal Year 2002*, Historical Tables Table 5.1: <http://www.gpoaccess.gov/usbudget/fy02/hist.html>.

42. Jason Furman (2005), *Top Ten Facts On Social Security's 70th Anniversary* (August 11), Center on Budget and Policy Priorities: <http://www.cbpp.org/8-11-05socsec.htm>.

43. Urban-Brookings Tax Policy Center (2005), "Historical Payroll Tax Rates" *Tax Facts*, Payroll/Tables: <http://taxpolicycenter.org/TaxFacts/TFDB/TFTemplate.cfm?Docid=45&Topic 2id=50>.

44. Isaac Shapiro, Allen Dupree, and James Sly (2001), *An Estimated 12 Million Low- and Moderate-Income Families—with 24 Million Children—Would Not Benefit From the Bush Tax*

Plan (February 7), Center on Budget and Policy Priorities: <http://www.cbpp.org/2-7 -01tax.pdf>.

45. Dean Baker and Mark Weisbrot (2000), *Social Security: The Phony Crisis* (Chicago: University of Chicago Press).

46. U.S. Social Security Administration (2005), *The 2005 Annual Report of the Board of Trustees of the Federal Old-Age and Survivors Insurance and Disability Insurance Trust Funds* (Washington, D.C.: U.S. Government Printing Office): <http://www.socialsecurity.gov/OACT/ TR/TR05/tr05.pdf>.

47. Chuck Collins, Chris Hartman, Karen Kraut, and Gloribell Mota (2004), *Shifty Tax Cuts: How They Move the Tax Burden off the Rich and onto Everyone Else*, United for a Fair Economy: <http://www.faireconomy.org/Taxes/HTMLReports/Shifty_Tax_Cuts.html>.

48. Bob Zahradnik and Joseph Llobrer (2004), *State Income Tax Burdens on Low-Income Families in 2003* (April 8), Center on Budget and Policy Priorities: <http://www.cbpp.org/4-8 -04sfp.htm>.

49. Institute on Taxation and Economic Policy (2003), *State and Local Taxes Hit Poor and Middle Class Far Harder Than the Wealthy* (January 7): <http://www.itepnet.org/wp2000/pr.pdf>.

50. Iris J. Lav (2004), *A Sales Tax Reduction Would Largely Benefit High-Income Tax Payers and Carry a High Cost* (July 19), Center for Budget and Policy Priorities: <http:// www.cbpp.org/6-8-04tax.htm>.

51. Nicholas Johns and David Tenney (2002), *The Rising Regressivity of State Taxes* (January 15), Center for Budget and Policy Priorities: <http://www.cbpp.org/1-15-02sfp.pdf>.

52. Ibid.

53. *See* Women's Social Policy and Research Center (2004), *Tax Reform and Tennessee Households: A Distributional Impact Analysis* and (2001), *Footing the Bill: Women and Tax Reform in Tennessee:* <http://sitemason.vanderbilt.edu/wsparc/home>.

54. Center for Policy Alternatives (2004), *Restoring the Promise of America: 2005 Progressive Agenda for the States* (December): <http://www.stateaction.org/publications/agenda/2005/ 2005agenda.pdf>.

55. Center on Budget and Policy Priorities (2004), *A Brief Update on State Fiscal Conditions and the Effects of Federal Policies on State Budgets* (September 13): <http:// www.cbpp.org/9-13 -04sfp.htm>.

56. Ibid.

57. Shawn Fremstad, Sharon Parrott, and Arloc Sherman (2004) *Unemployment Insurance Does Not Explain Why TANF Caseloads Are Falling as Poverty and Need are Rising* (October 12), Center on Budget and Policy Priorities: <http://www.cbpp.org/10-12-04tanf.htm>.

58. U.S. Congressional Budget Office (2004), *Effective Federal Tax Rates Under Current Law, 2001 to 2014:* <http://www.cbo.gov/showdoc.cfm?index=5746&sequence=1&from=0>.

59. David Kamin and Isaac Shapiro (2004), *Studies Shed New Light on Effects of Administration's Tax Cut* (September 13), Center on Budget and Policy Priorities: <http:// www.cbpp.org/8-25-04tax.pdf>.

60. National Women's Law Center (2001), *Women and Children Last: The Bush Tax Cut Plan* (March 5): <http://www.nwlc.org/pdf/womentax2.pdf>.

61. Ibid.

62. George W. Bush (2001), Radio Address by the President to the Nation (February 3): <http://www.whitehouse.gov/news/radio/20010203.html>.

63. Isaac Shapiro and Joel Friedman (2004). *Tax Returns: A Comprehensive Analysis of the Bush Administration Tax Cuts*, Center for Budget and Policy Priorities: <http://www.cbpp.org/4-23-04tax.pdf>.

64. Urban-Brookings Tax Policy Center (2004), Estimates/Distribution Tables T04-0057–T04-0062: <http://www.taxpolicycenter.org/TaxModel/tmdb/TMTemplate.cfm?template=simulation&SimID=18&relTTN=T04-0057>.

65. National Women's Law Center (2005), "New Census Data Show Women's Poverty Increases for Fourth Year, Women's Wages Decrease, Despite Economic Recovery," news release (August 30): <http://www.nwlc.org/details.cfm?id=2385&section=newsroom>.

66. National Women's Law Center (2001) *Women and Children Last: The Bush Tax Cut Plan* (March 5): <http://www.nwlc.org/pdf/womentax2.pdf>.

67. George W. Bush (2003), Radio Address by the President to the Nation (January 18): <http://www.whitehouse.gov/news/radio/20030118.html>.

68. Samantha Xu (2003), "Effects of Tax Cuts on Small Business Uncertain," *Women's eNews* (July 8): <http://www.womensenews.org/article.cfm/dyn/aid/1420/context/archive>.

69. Andrew Lee (2003), *President's Radio Address and Other Administration Statement Exaggerate Tax Plan's Impact on Small Business* (January 21), Center on Budget and Policy Priorities: <http://www.cbpp.org/1-18-03tax.htm>.

70. Samantha Xu (2003), "Effects of Tax Cuts on Small Business Uncertain," *Women's eNews* (July 8): <http://www.womensenews.org/article.cfm/dyn/aid/1420/context/archive>.

71. U.S. Congress, Joint Economic Committee (2001), *The Alternative Minimum Tax For Individuals: A Growing Burden* (May): <http://www.house.gov/jec/tax/amt.htm>.

72. James Horney (2005), *Repealing the Alternative Minimum Tax Without Offsetting the Cost Would Add $1.4 Trillion to the Federal Debt Over the Next Decade* (June 9), Center for Budget and Policy Priorities <http://www.cbpp.org/6-9-05tax.htm>.

73. U.S. Congress, Joint Economic Committee (2001), *The Alternative Minimum Tax For Individuals: A Growing Burden* (May): <http://www.house.gov/jec/tax/amt.htm>.

74. James Horney (2005), *Repealing the Alternative Minimum Tax Without Offsetting the Cost Would Add $1.4 Trillion to the Federal Debt Over the Next Decade* (June 9), Center for Budget and Policy Priorities <http://www.cbpp.org/6-9-05tax.htm>.

75. Ibid.

76. Ibid.

77. Ibid.

78. Leonard E. Burman, William G. Gale, Jeff Rohaly, and Matthew Hall (2004). *Key Points to the Alternative Minimum Tax*, Urban-Brookings Tax Policy Center: <http://www.brookings.edu/views/op-ed/gale/20040121amt.htm>.

79. Ibid.

80. David Cay Johnston (2003), *Perfectly Legal: The Covert Campaign to Rig Our Tax System to Benefit the Super Rich —and Cheat Everyone* Else (New York: Portfolio), 112.

81. Ibid.

82. Andrew Chamberlain and Patrick Fleenor (2005), *Backgrounder on the Individual Alternative Minimum Tax* (May 24), Tax Foundation: <http://www.taxfoundation.org/publications/show/498.html>.

83. David Cay Johnston (2003), *Perfectly Legal: The Covert Campaign to Rig Our Tax System to Benefit the Super Rich —and Cheat Everyone Else* (New York: Portfolio), 99.

84. Leonard E. Burman, William G. Gale, Jeff Rohaly, and Benjamin H. Harris (2002), *The Individual AMT: Problems and Potential Solutions*, Discussion Paper No. 5 (September 18), Urban-Brookings Tax Policy Center: <http://taxpolicycenter.org/publications/template.cfm?PubID=7912>.

85. James Horney (2005), *Repealing the Alternative Minimum Tax Without Offsetting the Cost Would Add $1.4 Trillion to the Federal Debt Over the Next Decade* (June 9), Center for Budget and Policy Priorities <http://www.cbpp.org/6-9-05tax.htm>.

86. David Cay Johnston (2003), *Perfectly Legal: The Covert Campaign to Rig Our Tax System to Benefit the Super Rich —and Cheat Everyone Else* (New York: Portfolio), 111.

87. James Horney (2005). *Repealing the Alternative Minimum Tax Without Offsetting the Cost Would Add $1.4 Trillion to the Federal Debt Over the Next Decade* (June 9), Center for Budget and Policy Priorities <http://www.cbpp.org/6-9-05tax.htm>.

88. Leonard E. Burman, William G. Gale, Jeff Rohaly, Benjamin H. Harris (2002), *The Individual AMT: Problems and Potential Solutions*. Tax Policy Center [online]: <http://taxpolicycenter.org/publications/template.cfm?PubID=7912>.

89. Leonard E. Burman, William G. Gale, Jeff Rohaly, and Benjamin H. Harris (2002), *The Individual AMT: Problems and Potential Solutions*, Discussion Paper No. 5 (September 18), Urban-Brookings Tax Policy Center: <http://taxpolicycenter.org/publications/template.cfm? PubID=7912>.

90. Bill Beach, Rea Hederman, and Tim Kane (2004), *The 2003 Tax Cuts and the Economy: A One-Year Assessment*, WebMemo #543 (July 21), Heritage Foundation: <http://www.heritage.org/Research/Taxes/wm543.cfm>.

91. Sylvia Allegretto, Jared Bernstein, and Isaac Shapiro (2005), *The Lukewarm 2004 Labor Market: Despite Some Signs of Improvement, Wages Fell, Job Growth Lagged, and Unemployment Spells Remained Long* (February 16), Center on Budget and Policy Priorities and Economic Policy Institute: <http://www.cbpp.org/2-16-05ui.htm>.

92. David Kamin and Isaac Shapiro (2004), *Studies Shed New Light on Effects of Administration's Tax Cut* (September 13), Center on Budget and Policy Priorities: <http://www. cbpp.org/8-25-04tax.pdf>.

93. Martin Mühleisen and Christopher Towe (2004), *U.S. Fiscal Policies and Priorities for Long Run Sustainability* (January 7), International Monetary Fund: <http://www.imf.org/external/Pubs/NFT/Op/227/#overview>.

94. Marty Liebowitz (2003), *Winning Responses to Tough Tax Questions*, United for a Fair Economy (May 12): <http://www.ufenet.org/econ/state/Talking_Taxes>.

5   HOW TODAY'S POLICIES HURT WOMEN, CHILDREN, AND FAMILIES

1. Heidi Hartmann (2004), presentation at "Women's Voices Matter: Women Elect to Speak," annual conference of the National Council for Research on Women, June 6–7, Washington, D.C.

2. Chuck Collins, Chris Hartman, Karen Kraut, and Gloribell Mota (2004), *Shifty Tax Cuts: How They Move the Tax Burden off the Rich and onto Everyone Else*, United for a Fair Economy: <http://www.faireconomy.org/Taxes/HTMLReports/Shifty_Tax_Cuts.html>.

3. U.S. Congressional Budget Office (2004), *The Budget and Economic Outlook: Fiscal Years 2005–2014*, Chapter 4: <http://www.cbo.gov/showdoc.cfm?index=6060&sequence=5>.

4. Chuck Collins, Chris Hartman, Karen Kraut, and Gloribell Mota (2004), *Shifty Tax Cuts: How They Move the Tax Burden off the Rich and onto Everyone Else*, United for a Fair Economy: <http://www.faireconomy.org/Taxes/HTMLReports/Shifty_Tax_Cuts.html>.

5. Citizens for Tax Justice (2004), *Overall Tax Rates Have Flattened Sharply Under Bush* (April 13): <http://www.ctj.org/pdf/fsl2004.pdf>.

6. Robert Greenstein and Isaac Shapiro (2003), *The New Definitive CBO Data on Income and Tax Trends* (September 23), Center on Budget and Policy Priorities: <http://www.cbpp.org/9-23-03tax.htm>.

7. Isaac Shapiro (2005), *What New CBO Data Indicate About Long-term Income Distribution Trends* (March 7), Center on Budget and Policy Priorities: <http://www.cbpp.org/3-7-05tax.htm>.

8. David Kamin and Isaac Shapiro (2004), *Studies Shed New Light on Effects of Administration's Tax Cut* (September 13), Center on Budget and Policy Priorities: <http://www.cbpp.org/8-25-04tax.pdf>.

9. Robert Greenstein and Isaac Shapiro (2003), *The New Definitive CBO Data on Income and Tax Trends* (September 23), Center on Budget and Policy Priorities: <http://www.cbpp.org/9-23-03tax.htm>.

10. Isaac Shapiro (2005), *What New CBO Data Indicate About Long-term Income Distribution Trends* (March 7), Center on Budget and Policy Priorities: <http://www.cbpp.org/3-7-05tax.htm>.

11. Center on Budget and Policy Priorities (2005), *Economic Recovery Failed to Benefit Much of the Population in 2004*, (August 30): <http://www.cbpp.org/8-30-05pov.htm>.

12. Inequality.org (2004), *How Unequal Are We, Anyway? A Statistical Briefing Book*: <http://inequality.org/facts.html>.

13. Consumer Federation of America (2004), *Research Shows That Women on Their Own Face Financial Challenges* (January 12): <http://www.consumerfed.org/womenfinance.pdf>.

14. Inequality.org (2004), *How Unequal Are We, Anyway? A Statistical Briefing Book*: <http://inequality.org/facts.html>.

15. David Kamin and Richard Kogan (2004), *Deficit Picture Grimmer Than CBO's March Projections Suggest* (June 4), Center on Budget and Policy Priorities: <http://www.cbpp.org/6-4-04bud.htm>.

16. Joel Friedman, Ruth Carlitz, and David Kamin (2005). *Extending the Tax Cuts Would Cost $2.1 Trillion Through 2015* (February 9), Center for Budget and Policy Priorities: <http://www.cbpp.org/2-2-05tax.htm>.

17. Joan Entmacher (2004), presentation at "Women's Voices Matter: Women Elect to Speak," annual conference of the National Council for Research on Women, 6–7 June 2004, Washington, D.C.

18. Richard Kogan and Robert Greenstein (2004), *Official Treasury Report Shows Fourth*

Year of Deficit Growth Despite Economic Recovery (October 4), Center on Budget and Policy Priorities: <http://www.cbpp.org/10-14-04bud.htm>.

19. Isaac Shapiro and Joel Friedman (2004). *Tax Returns: A Comprehensive Analysis of the Bush Administration Tax Cuts*, Center for Budget and Policy Priorities: <http://www.cbpp.org/4-23-04tax.pdf>.

20. U.S. Office of Management and Budget (2005), *Budget of the United States Government, Fiscal Year 2006*, Historical Tables, Tables 13 and 7.1: <http://www.whitehouse.gov/omb/budget/fy2006/pdf/hist.pdf>.

21. David Kamin and Richard Kogan (2004), *Deficit Picture Grimmer Than CBO's March Projections Suggest* (June 4), Center on Budget and Policy Priorities: <http://www.cbpp.org/6-4-04bud.htm>.

22. U.S. Executive Office of the President (2003), *Budget of the United States Government, Fiscal Year 2004*, Historical Tables 1.3–2.3, 25–34 <http://www.gpoaccess.gov/usbudget/fy04/pdf/hist.pdf>.

23. U.S. Congressional Budget Office (2004), *The Budget and Economic Outlook: Fiscal Years 2005–2014*, Table F-10: <http://www.cbo.gov/showdoc.cfm?index=4985&sequence=0>.

24. Richard Kogan and David Kamin (2004), *President's Budget Contains Large Cuts in Domestic Discretionary Programs* (June 7), Center on Budget and Policy Priorities: <http://www.cbpp.org/2-5-04bud.htm>.

25. Heidi Hartmann (2004), presentation at "Women's Voices Matter: Women Elect to Speak," annual conference of the National Council for Research on Women, 6–7 June 2004, Washington, D.C.

26. Richard Kogan and David Kamin (2004), *President's Budget Contains Large Cuts in Domestic Discretionary Programs* (June 7), Center on Budget and Policy Priorities: <http://www.cbpp.org/2-5-04bud.htm>.

27. Center on Budget and Policy Priorities (2004), *Broad Cuts in Domestic Programs After 2005 Under Administration Budget* (March 5): <http://www.cbpp.org/2-27-04bud-fact.htm>.

28. C. Eugene Steuerle (2003), *The Incredible Shrinking Budget for Working Families and Children* (December 1), Urban Institute: <http://www.urban.org/url.cfm?ID=310914>.

6 WHY WOMEN FEEL MORE STING FROM SERVICE CUTS

1. Intuit.com (2002) *"MORE" Women Take Control of Their Taxes*, report on survey results (March 21): <http://www.intuit.com/about_intuit/press_releases/2002/03-21.html>.

2. ABC News/*Washington Post*, (2003), commissioned telephone survey of 1,105 adults, including an oversample of 169 Blacks, conducted on April 27–30 by TNS Intersearch. (Question: "What is your preference—to have the federal government cut taxes or to have the federal government spend more on domestic programs such as education, health care and Social Security?" Cut taxes: 29 percent; Spend more: 68 percent; Neither: 1 percent; No opinion: 2 percent. Percentages may not add to 100 percent because of rounding.): <http://www.publicagenda.org/issues/major_proposals_detail.cfm?issue_type=federal_budget&list=3>.

3. National Council of La Raza (2004), *Latinos Optimistic About Their Future, Feel Candidates Ignore their Issues, Survey Finds*, news release (June 27): <http://www.nclr.org/content/news/detail/25333>.

4. R. Michael Alvarez and Edward McCaffery (2000), *Is There a Gender Gap in Fiscal Political Preferences?* Working Paper No. 1, Center for the Study of Law and Politics, USC Law School and California Institute of Technology: <http://lawweb.usc.edu/cslp/pages/documents/alvarez_mccaffery_000.pdf>.

5. National Council for Research on Women (2005), commissioned national telephone survey of 800 women and 400 men ages 18 and older, conducted on March 23–29, designed and administered by Lake Snell Perry Mermin & Associates; margin of error for entire survey +/–3.4 percent.

6. National Council of Women's Organizations, Child Care Task Force (2004), *Testimony Submitted to the Democratic and Republican Party Platform Committees* (June 14): <http://www.familyinitiative.org/ptestimony.htm>.

7. Legal Momentum, Family Initiative (2005), *Issues and Analysis—Afterschool:* <http://www.legalmomentum.org/fi/issues/afterschool/>

8. Kathy Rodgers (2004), text of statement at Congressional Briefing (June 22), Legal Momentum, Family Initiative: <http://www.familyinitiative.org/rodgersspeech.pdf>.

9. National Council of Women's Organizations, Child Care Task Force (2004), *Testimony Submitted to the Democratic and Republican Party Platform Committees* (June 14): <http://www.familyinitiative.org/ptestimony.htm>.

10. Fair Taxes for All (2005), *President's Budget Reflects Distorted Priorities*, news release (February 8): <http://www.nwlc.org/pdf/FTFA2-8-05BudgetRelease.pdf>.

11. National Head Start Association (2004), *The Dismantling of Head Start is Already Underway* (October 27): <http://www.nhsa.org/press/index_news_102704.htm>.

12. Ibid.

13. Anne E. Kornblut (2005), "The Presidents Budget: Education—A Cut for Schools, a First for Bush," *New York Times* (February 8), A21.

14. American Federation of State, County, and Municipal Employees (AFSCME) (2005), *President Bush's 2006 Budget Plan* (February 15): <http://www.afsc.org/economic-justice/sos/documents/afscme-analysis.pdf>.

15. National Women's Law Center (2004). *NWLC Calls on Bush Administration to Do More to Ensure Gender Equity in Vocational Education Programs* (February 12): <http://www.nwlc.org/details.cfm?id=1780&section=newsroom>.

16. Pew Hispanic Center (2004), *Latino Teens Staying in High School, A Challenge for All Generations,* Fact Sheet: <http://pewhispanic.org/files/factsheets/7.3.pdf>.

17. U.S. Congress, House, Committee on Education and the Work Force, Democratic Staff (2002), *President Bush's Budget: Failing to Meet the Needs of Historically Black Colleges* (February 12): <http://edworkforce.house.gov/democrats>.

18. Robert Pear (2005), "The President's Budget: Domestic Programs—Subject to Bush's Knife: Aid for Food and Heating," *New York Times* (February 8), A22.

19. Kaiser Family Foundation (2005), Daily Health Policy Report (August 31): <http://www.kaisernetwork.org/daily_reports/rep_index.cfm?hint=3&DR_ID=32334>.

20. Kaiser Family Foundation (2004), *Women's Health Policy Facts: Women's Health Insurance Coverage,* Fact Sheet (June): <http://www.kff.org/womenshealth/loader.cfm?url=/commonspot/security/getfile.cfm&PageID=37684>.

21. National Women's Law Center (2005), "New Census Data Show Women's Poverty Increases for Fourth Year, Women's Wages Decrease, Despite Economic Recovery," news release (August 30): <http://www.nwlc.org/details.cfm?id=2385&section=newsroom>.

22. Kaiser Family Foundation (2005), *Daily Health Policy Report* (August 31): <http://www.kaisernetwork.org/daily_reports/rep_index.cfm?hint=3&DR_ID=32334>.

23. Robert Greenstein (2004), *Number of Americans Without Insurance Reaches Highest Level on Record* (August 27), Center on Budget and Policy Priorities: <http://www.cbpp.org/8 -26-04health.htm>.

24. Office of U.S. Senator Tim Johnson (2003), *Johnson Says Native Americans Left Behind Under Proposed $550 Billion Tax Cut* (May 14): <http://johnson.senate.gov/~johnson/releases/ 200305/2003516752.html>.

25. American Psychological Association (2005), "FY 2006: A Funding Squeeze," *APA Monitor* 36: 4 (April): <http://www.apa.org/monitor/apr05/squeeze.html>.

26. U.S. Department of Health and Human Services (2003), *Medicaid Beneficiaries, Selected Fiscal Years:* <http://www.cms.hhs.gov/researchers/pubs/datacompendium/2003/03pg35.pdf>.

27. Kaiser Family Foundation (2004), *Women's Health Policy Facts: Women's Health Insurance Coverage,* Fact Sheet (June): <http://www.kff.org/womenshealth/loader.cfm?url=/ commonspot/security/getfile.cfm&PageID=37684>.

28. U.S. Congressional Budget Office (2004), *Financing Long-Term Care for the Elderly* <http://www.cbo.gov/showdoc.cfm?index=5400&sequence=0>.

29. National Women's Law Center (2003), *Don't Balance Medicare Reform on the Backs of Women:* <http://www.house.gov/schakowsky/11_19_03_NW_C_Medicare_Women.doc>.

30. Edwin Park, Melanie Nathanson, Robert Greenstein, and John Springer (2003), *The Troubling Medicare Legislation* (December 8), Center on Budget and Policy Priorities: <http://www.cbpp.org/11-18-03health2.htm>.

31. Edwin Park (2004), *Administration's Proposed Tax Credit for the Purchase of Health Insurance Could Weaken Employer-Based Health Insurance* (April 6), Center on Budget and Policy Priorities: <http://www.cbpp.org/2-18-04health2.htm>.

32. Edwin Park and Robert Greenstein (2004), *Proposal For New HSA Tax Deduction Found Likely to Increase the Ranks of the Uninsured* (July 22), Center on Budget and Policy Priorities: <http://www.cbpp.org/4-19-04health.htm>; and Edwin Park and Robert Greenstein (2004), *New Retirement Medical Account Proposal Would Create Lucrative Tax Shelter and Swell Deficits, But Do Little To Help Low- and Moderate-Income Seniors* (July 22), Center on Budget and Policy Priorities: <http://www.cbpp.org/4-19-04health.htm>.

33. National Women's Law Center (2004), *E-Update* (December 4): <http://nwlc.org/ details.cfm?id=2064&section=infocenter>.

34. U.S. House of Representatives, Democratic Policy Committee (2001). *The Bush Budget Shortchanges Women: Special Report* (March 29): <http://truthout.com/mm_01/4.DPC .women.pdf>.

35. National Women's Law Center (2002), *Women of Color Have Most to Lose if Social Security is Privatized* (May 21): <http://www.nwlc.org/details.cfm?id=1105&section=newsroom>.

36. U.S. House of Representatives, Democratic Policy Committee (2001). *The Bush Budget Shortchanges Women: Special Report* (March 29): <http://truthout.com/mm_01/4.DPC . women.pdf>.

37. National Women's Law Center (2002), *Women of Color Have Most to Lose if Social Security Is Privatized:* <http://www.nwlc.org/details.cfm?id=1105&section=newsroom>.

38. Paul Krugman (2004), "Inventing a Crisis," *New York Times* (December 7), A27.

39. Darcy Ann Olsen (1998), *Greater Financial Security for Women with Private Accounts,* Briefing Paper (July 28), Cato Institute: <http://www.socialsecurity.org/pubs/articles/bp-038.html>.

40. U.S. Social Security Administration (2005), *Social Security Income, Outgo, and Assets* (updated May 5): <http://www.ssa.gov/OACT/ProgData/assets.html>.

41. Alicia Munnell (1998), *Why Social Security Privatization Would Hurt Women,* Issue Brief (November), Carroll School of Management, Boston College: <http://www.socsec.org/facts/Issue_Briefs/PDF_versions/munell_women.PDF>.

42. Robert Greenstein, Peter Orszag, and Richard Kogan (2004), *The Implications of the Social Security Projections Issued by The Congressional Budget Office* (June 14), Center on Budget and Policy Priorities: <http://www.cbpp.org/6-14-04bud.htm>.

43. Paul Krugman (2004), "Inventing a Crisis," *New York Times* (December 7), A27.

44. Susan Rees, McAuley Institute (2003), "Women and Housing: A Status Report," *Step Up* 7:2 <http://www.housingall.com/STEPUP/Women_Housing.htm>.

45. Center for Budget and Policy Priorities (2004), *Response to HUD Secretary Jackson's New York Times Column on Housing Voucher* (August 16): <http://www.cbpp.org/8-16-04hous.htm>.

46. Edmund L. Andrews (2005), "White House Budget Projections Suggest Pain, Much of It Political," *New York Times* (February 11), A23.

47. American Federation of State, County, and Municipal Employees (AFSCME) (2005), *President Bush's 2006 Budget Plan* (February 15): <http://www.afsc.org/economic-justice/sos/documents/afscme-analysis.pdf>.

48. Karen Cunnygham and Beth Brown (2004), *Characteristics of Food Stamp Households: Fiscal Year 2003,* Office of Analysis, Nutrition, and Evaluation: <http://www.mathematica-mpr.com/publications/PDFs/2003Characteristics.pdf>.

49. Karen Cunnygham and Beth Brown (2004), *Characteristics of Food Stamp Households: Fiscal Year 2003,* Office of Analysis, Nutrition, and Evaluation: <http://www.mathematica-mpr.com/publications/PDFs/2003Characteristics.pdf>.

50. Paul Krugman (2004), "Bush's Class-War Budget," *New York Times* (February 11), A25.

51. Center on Budget and Policy Priorities (2004), *One in Nine Households at Risk of Hunger* (December 20): <http://www.cbpp.org/12-20-04pov-pr.htm>.

52. Edmund L. Andrews (2005), "White House Budget Projections Suggest Pain, Much of It Political," *New York Times* (February 11), A23.

53. Robert Pear (2005), "The President's Budget: Domestic Programs—Subject to Bush's Knife: Aid for Food and Heating," *New York Times* (February 8), A22.

54. Elizabeth Olson (2005), "Fears for a Program that Lends Just a Little: Budget Cuts Imperil S.B.A.'s Microloans," *New York Times* (March 17), C7.

55. National Women's Law Center (2005), "New Census Data Show Women's Poverty Increases for Fourth Year, Women's Wages Decrease, Despite Economic Recovery," news release (August 30): <http://www.nwlc.org/details.cfm?id=2385&section=newsroom>.

56. Ibid.

57. Pamela Loprest (2003), *Fewer Welfare Leavers Employed in Weak Economy* (August 21), Urban Institute: <http://www.urban.org/template.cfm?Template=/TaggedContent/ViewPublication . cfm&PublicationID=8550&NavMenuID=95>.

58. "Majority" is used here because roughly 11 percent of immigrants classified as "humanitarian" immigrants (refugees and people granted asylum) are allowed access to some of these services. Audrey Singer, *Welfare Reform and Immigrants: A Policy Review*, Brookings Institution: <http://www.brook.edu/dybdocroot/urban/pubs/200405_singer.pdf>.

59. U.S. Bureau of Labor Statistics (2004), *Household Data Annual Averages:* <http://www.bls.gov/cps/cpsaat15.pdf>.

60. Paula England (1992), *Comparable Worth: Theories and Evidence* (New York: Aldine de Gruyter).

61. Annette Bernhardt, Laura Dresser, and Catherine Hill (2000), *Why Privatizing Government Services Would Hurt Women Workers*, Research-in-Brief, Institute for Women's Policy Research: <http://www.iwpr.org/pdf/b237.pdf>.

62. U.S. Department of Labor, Women's Bureau (2003), *20 Leading Occupations of Women*, based on data from Bureau of Labor Statistics: <http://www.dol.gov/wb/factsheets/20lead2003 _ txt.htm>.

7   REAL WOMEN NEED REAL TAX REFORM: A CALL TO ACTION

1. Noeleen Heyzer (2005), remarks at "Women Who Make a Difference," NCRW annual awards dinner, afternoon program, May 1, New York.

2. Cabral Escobedo (2005), "Remarks of U.S. Treasurer Anna Escobedo Cabral, Go Direct Partnership Recognition Event," March 16, Chicago, IL: <http://www.treas.gov/press/releases/ js2319.htm>.

FORUM: VIEWS FROM THE COUNCIL'S NETWORK OF CENTERS

1. Leslie J. Calman and Linda Tarr-Whelan (2005), *Early Child Education for All: A Wise Investment*, recommendations arising from a conference sponsored by Legal Momentum's Family Initiative and the MIT Workplace Center, December 9–10, 2004, Cambridge, MA: <http://www.legalmomentum.org/fi/pdf/FamilyInitiativeReport.pdf>.

2. Girls Incorporated (2000) *Taking the Lead: Girls' Rights in the 21st Century:* <http://www.girlsinc.org/ic/content/HarrisPollBookRev311.pdf>.

3. College Board (2004), *Trends in Student Aid 2004; Trends in Student Pricing 2004:* <http://www.collegeboard.com/splash>.

4. Ruth Pearson (2003), "Feminist Responses to Economic Globalization," *Gender and Development* 11: 1: <http://www.awid.org/publications/gen_dev/pearson.pdf>.

The Feminist Press at the City University of New York is a nonprofit literary and educational institution dedicated to publishing work by and about women. Our existence is grounded in the knowledge that women's writing has often been absent or underrepresented on bookstore and library shelves and in educational curricula—and that such absences contribute, in turn, to the exclusion of women from the literary canon, from the historical record, and from the public discourse.

The Feminist Press was founded in 1970. In its early decades, the Press launched the contemporary rediscovery of "lost" American women writers, and went on to diversify its list by publishing significant works by American women writers of color. More recently, the Press's publishing program has focused on international women writers, who remain far less likely to be translated than male writers, and on nonfiction works that explore issues affecting the lives of women around the world.

Founded in an activist spirit, the Feminist Press is currently undertaking initiatives that will bring its books and educational resources to under-served populations, including community colleges, public high schools and middle schools, literacy and ESL programs, and prison education programs. As we move forward into the twenty-first century, we continue to expand our work to respond to women's silences wherever they are found.

For a complete catalog of the Press's 250 books, please refer to our website: www.feministpress.org.